Silesian Folk Tales Coloring Book: Intricate Vintage Illustrations

Publisher's notes:

Silesian Folk Tales Coloring Book: Intricate Vintage Illustrations, copyright Mix Books, LLC, 2014

Mix-BooksOnline.com

Manufactured in the United States.

Introduction:

These prints, by C. F. Arcier are from the classic book of folklore, Silesian Folk Tales (The Book of Rübezahl), first printed in 1915, by James Lee and James Thomas Carey. Create stunning hand-colored images of Rubezahl - the spirit prince who can make himself incredibly beautiful or hideously ugly - and the other characters in these classic tales.

Illustrations are printed on every other page (leaving the back side of the page blank) so that colors do not interfere with other pictures. It is also recommended that you place an extra sheet of paper between the pages to prevent any bleed, then your completed work can be admired to perfection, or even cut out and framed.

Because of their age the original illustrations have been restored to be suitable for coloring. Please keep in mind, however, there may still be imperfections.

The illustrations depict scenes from tales that have their roots in Silesia, a region in Poland with a checkered history of possession by the Bohemian crown, the Austrian Habsburgs and Prussia.

Silesian Folk Tales (The Book of Rübezahl) is in the Public Domain.

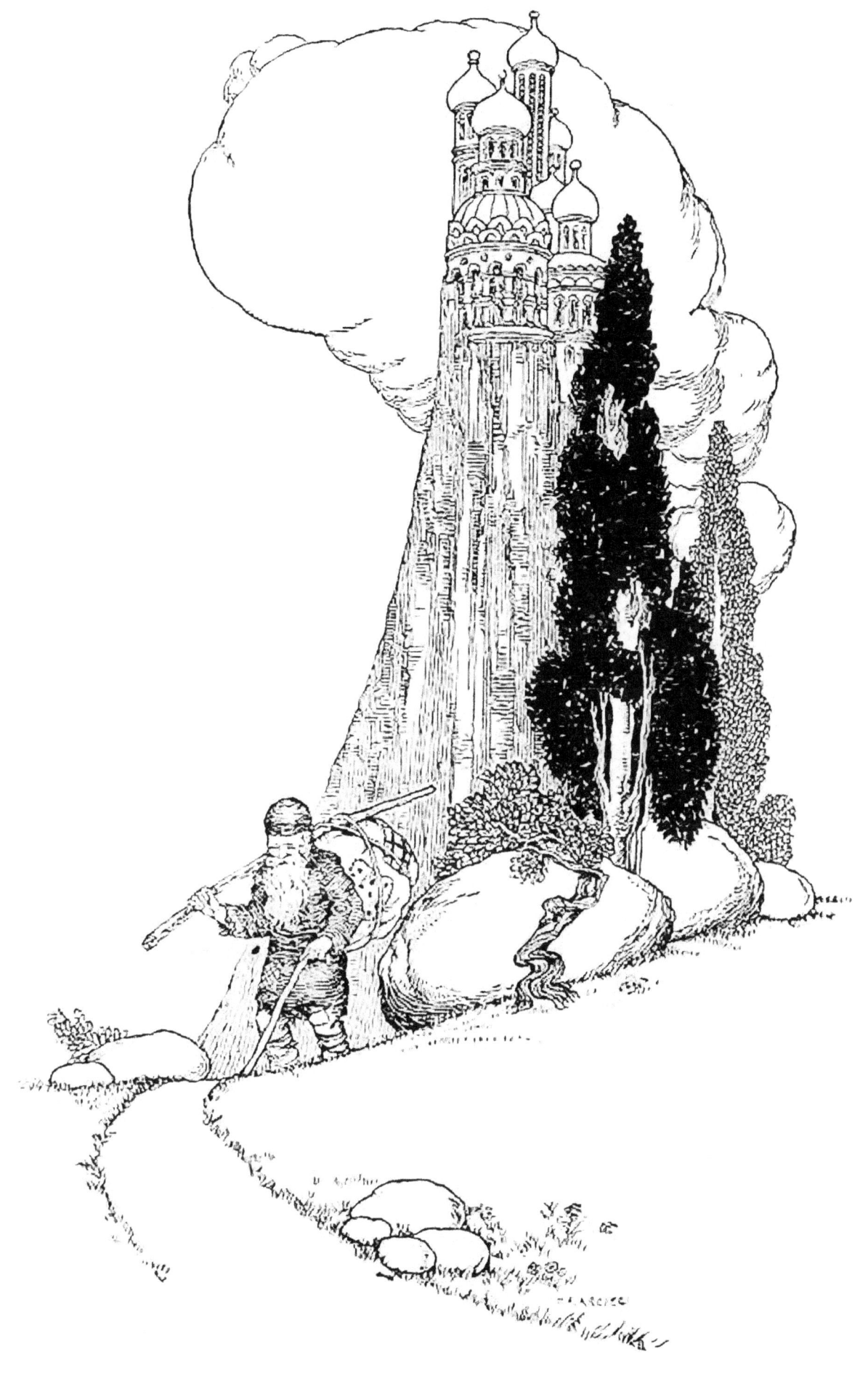

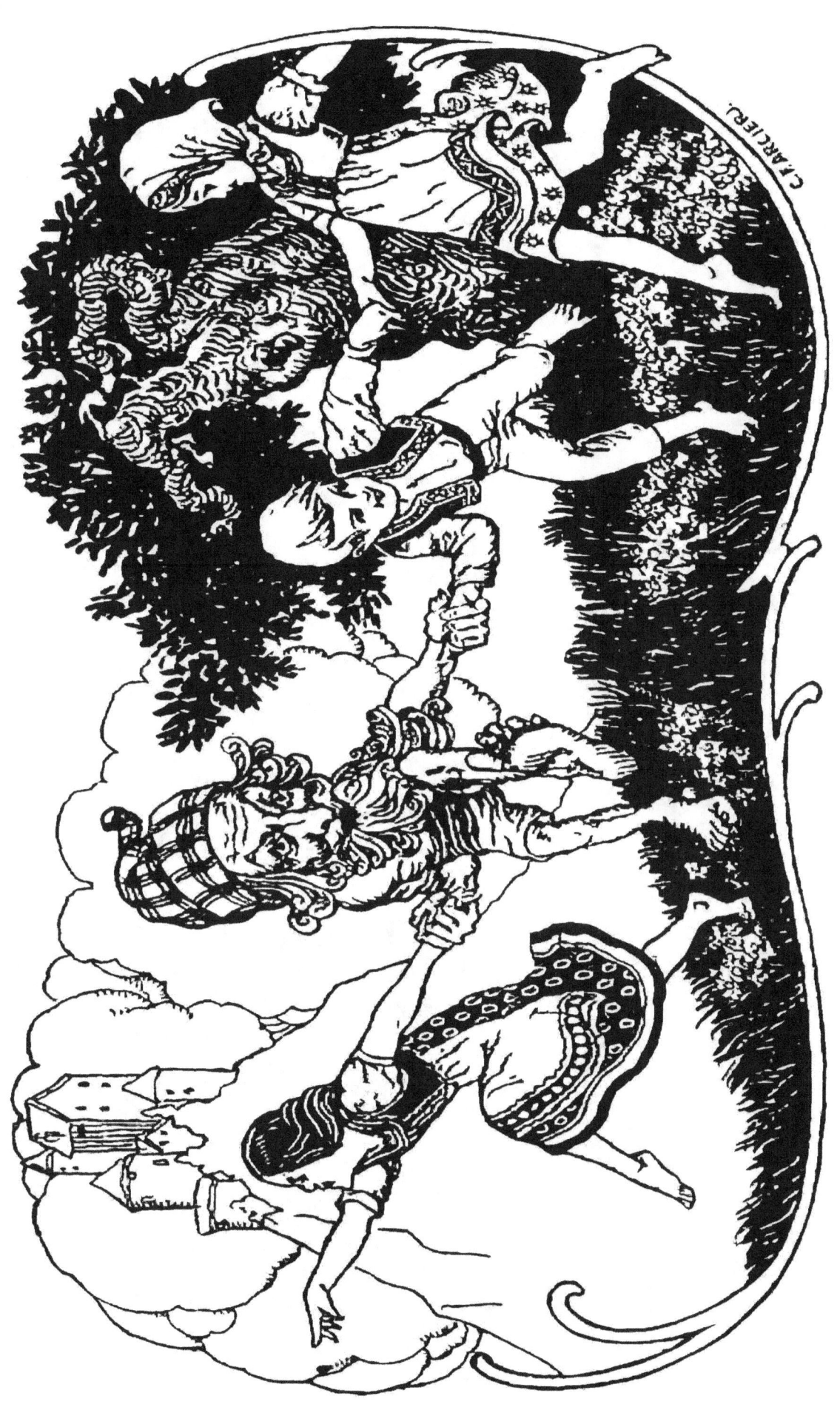

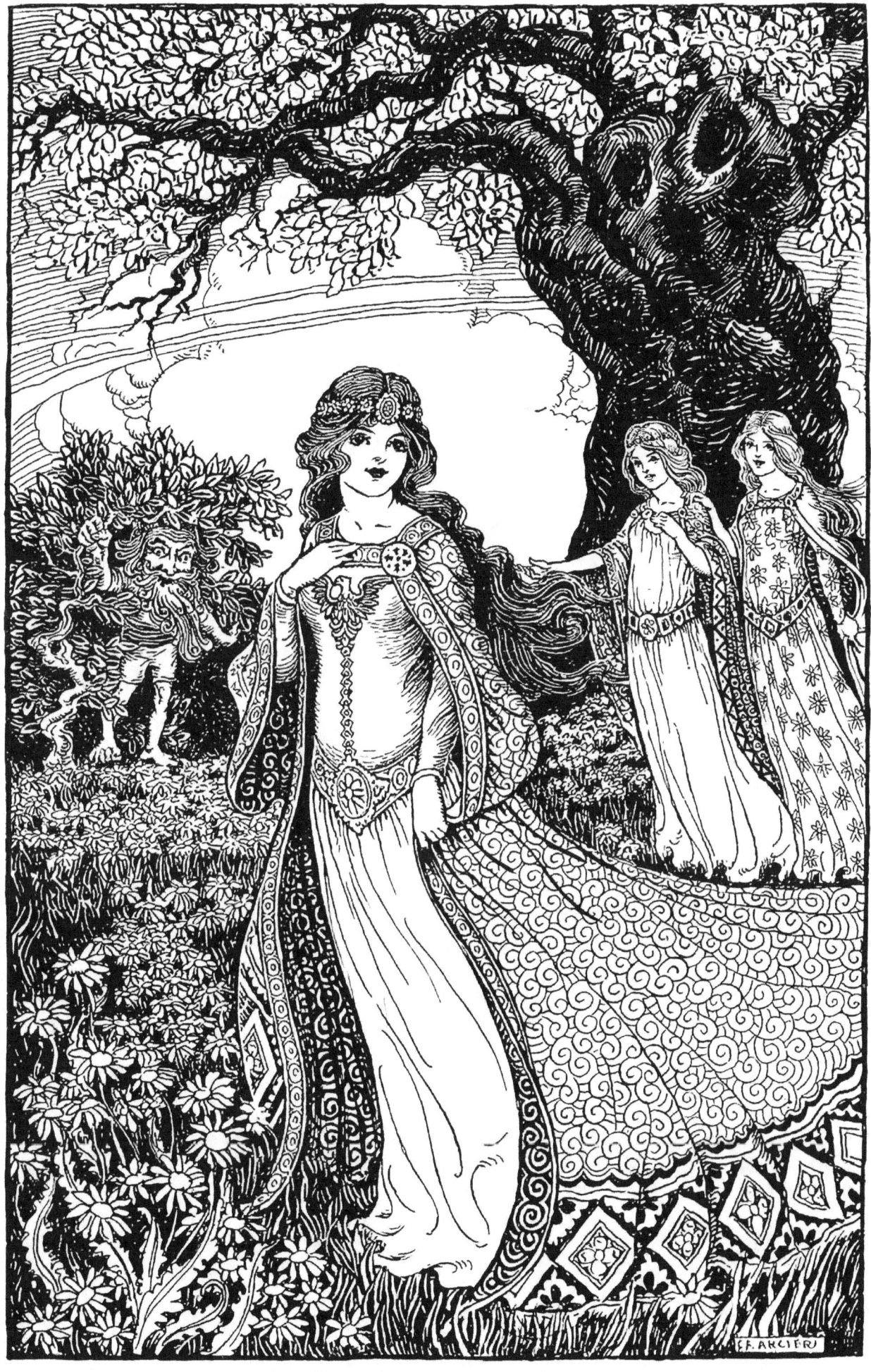

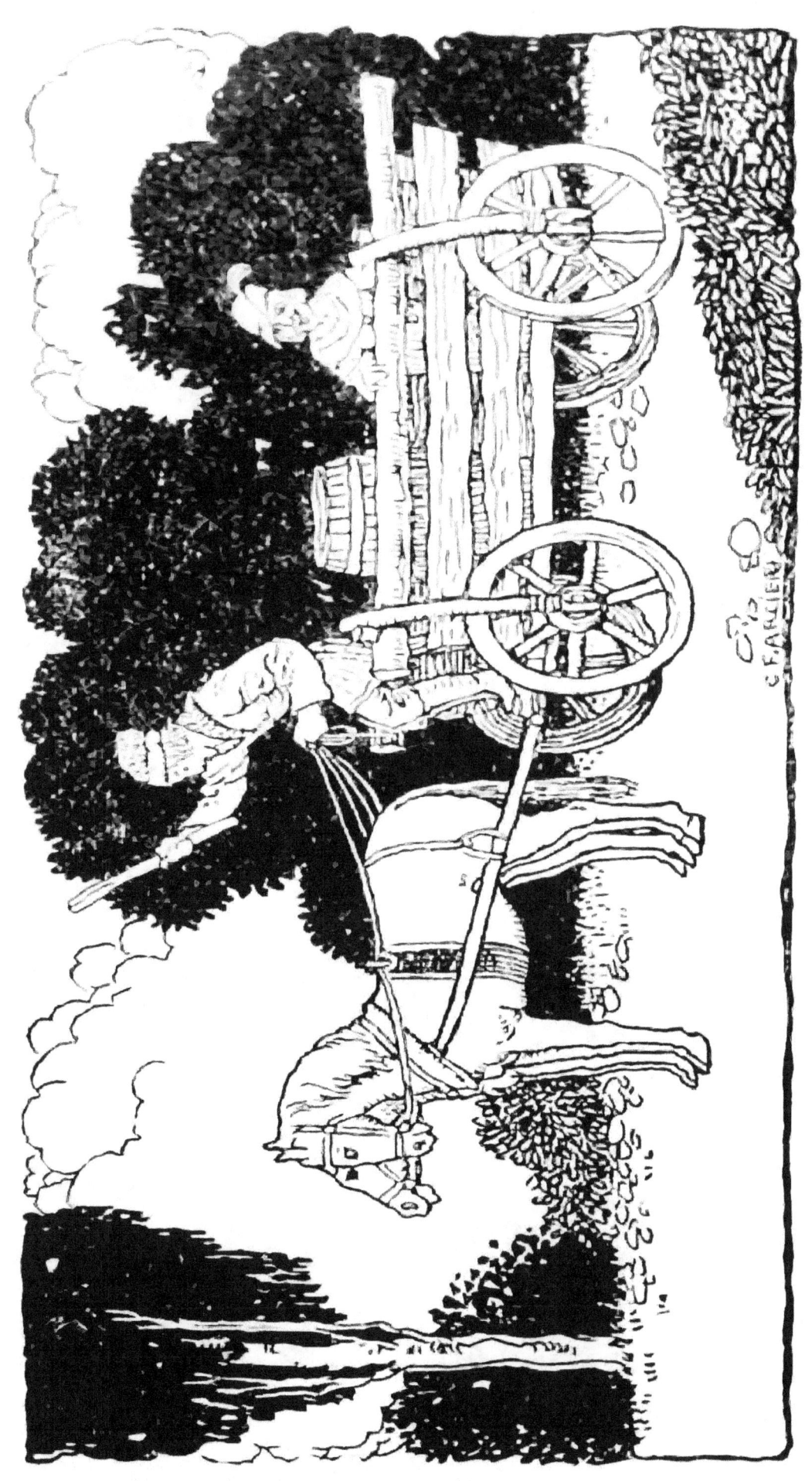

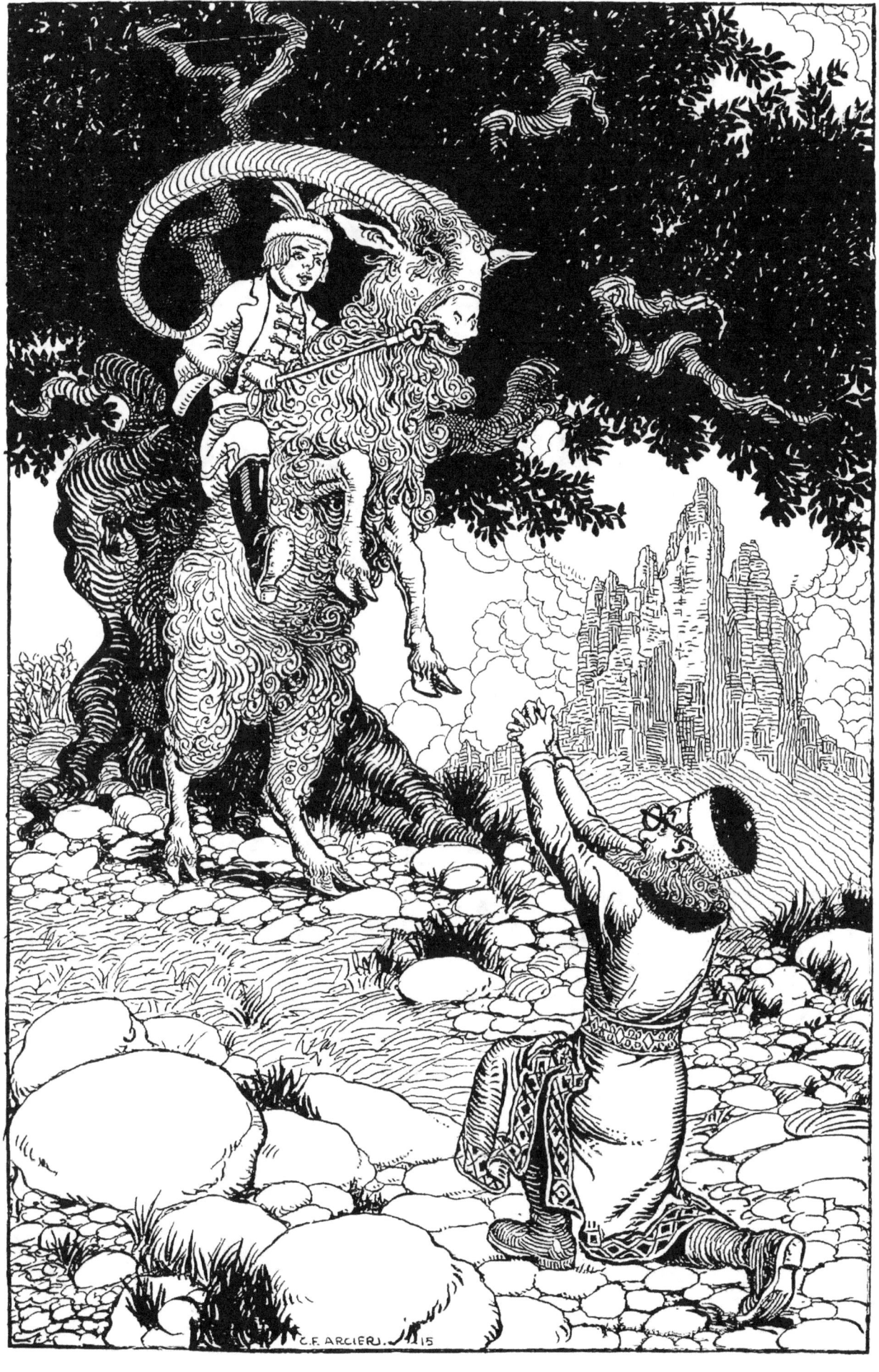

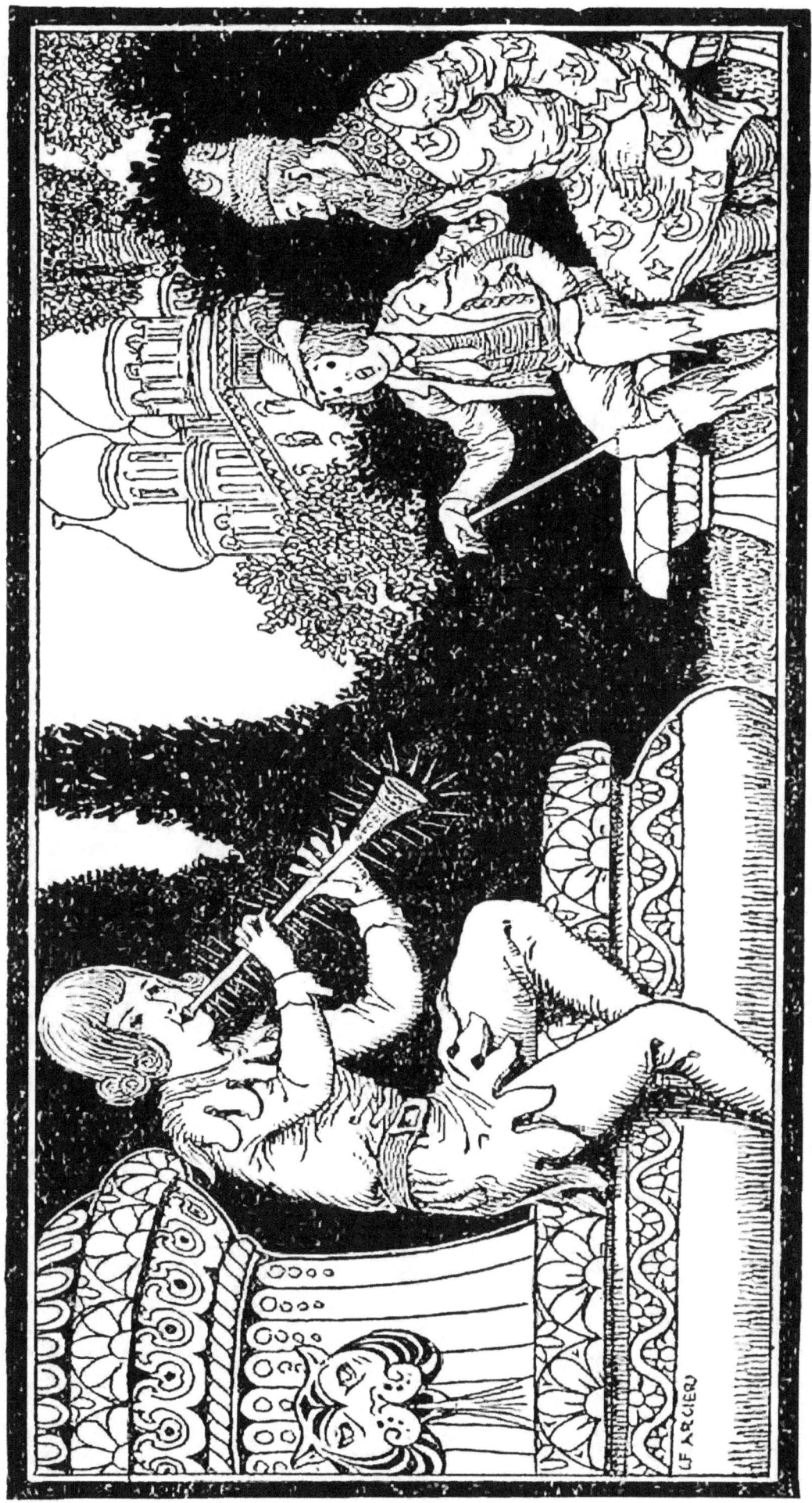

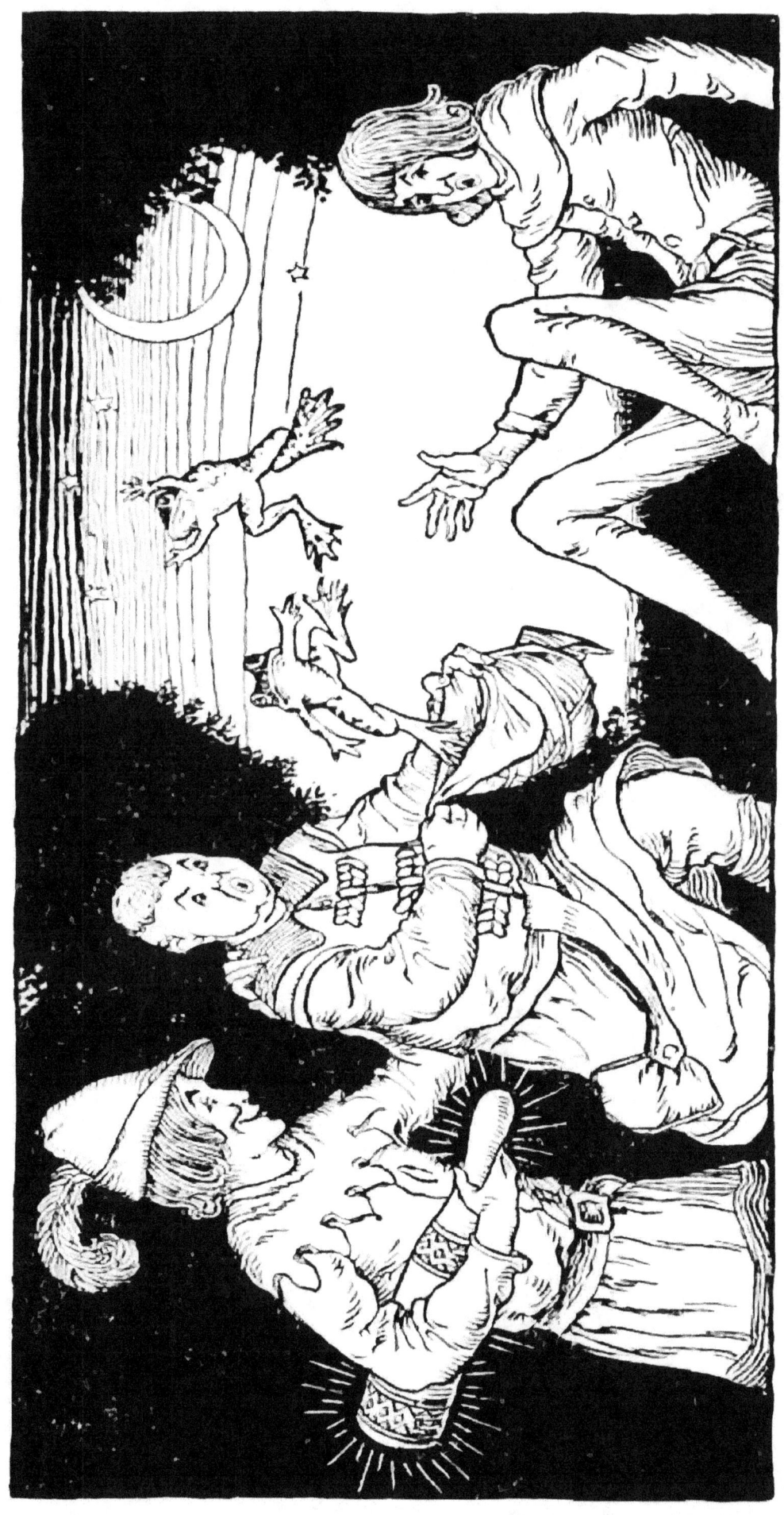

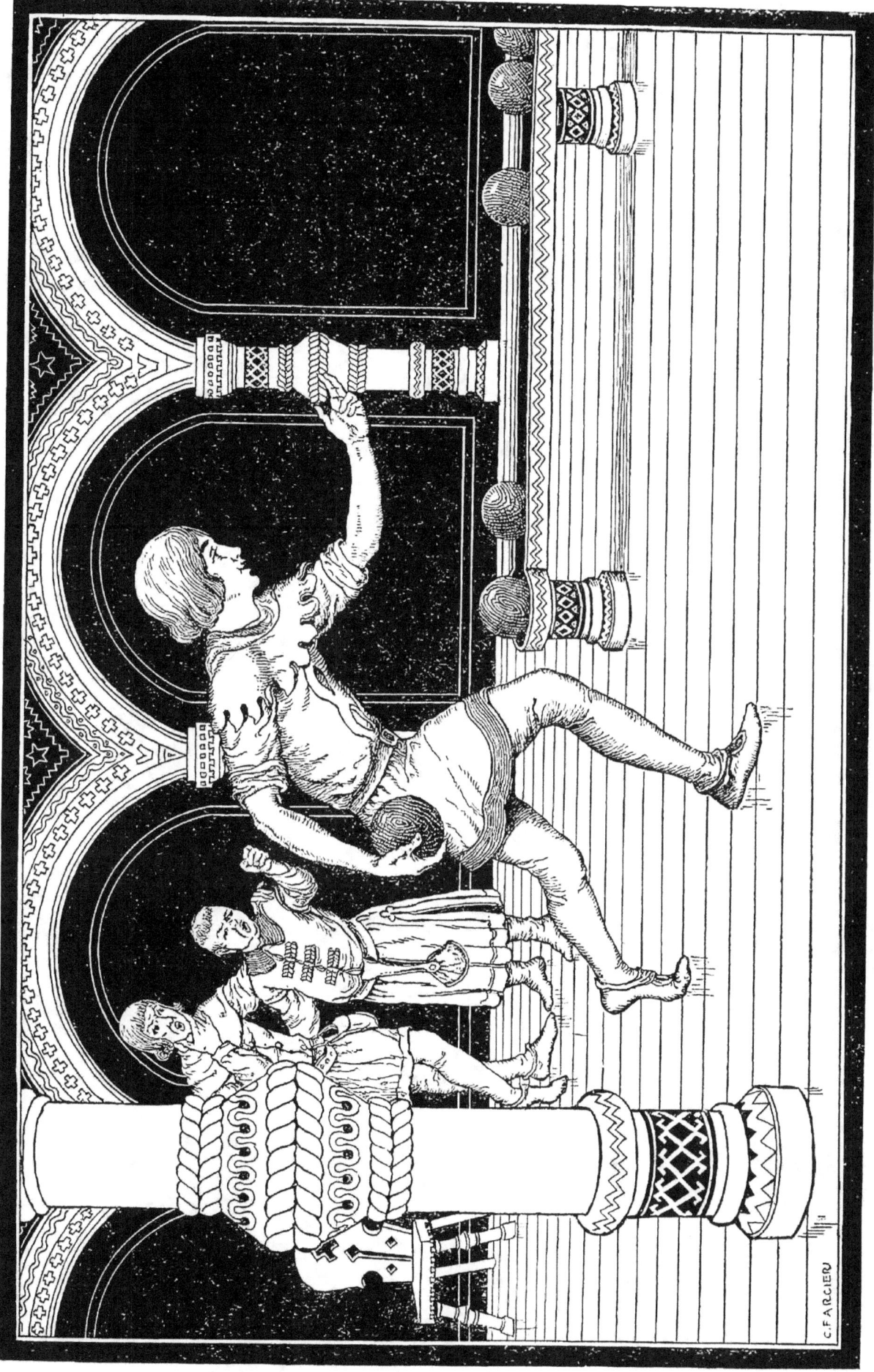

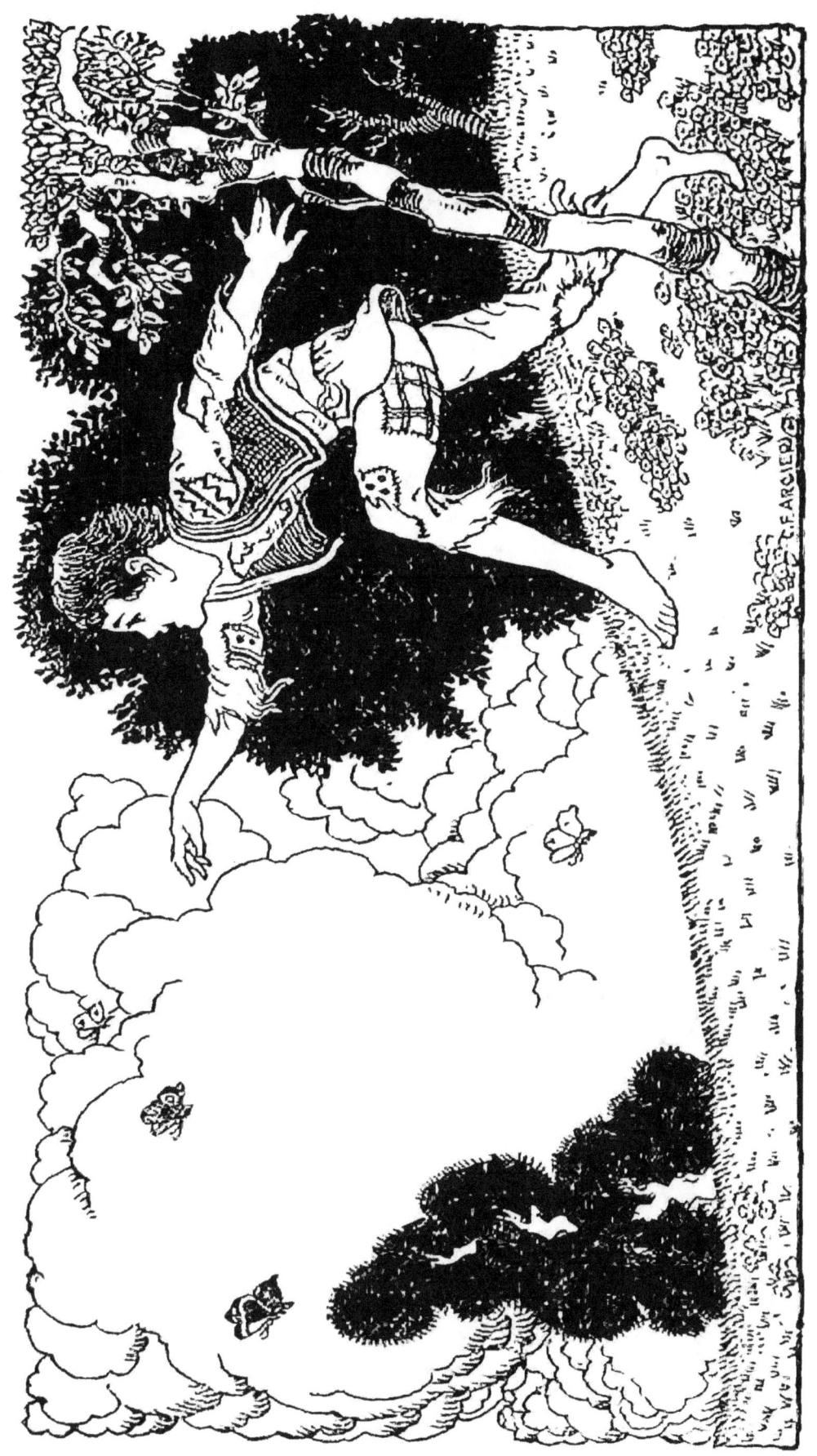

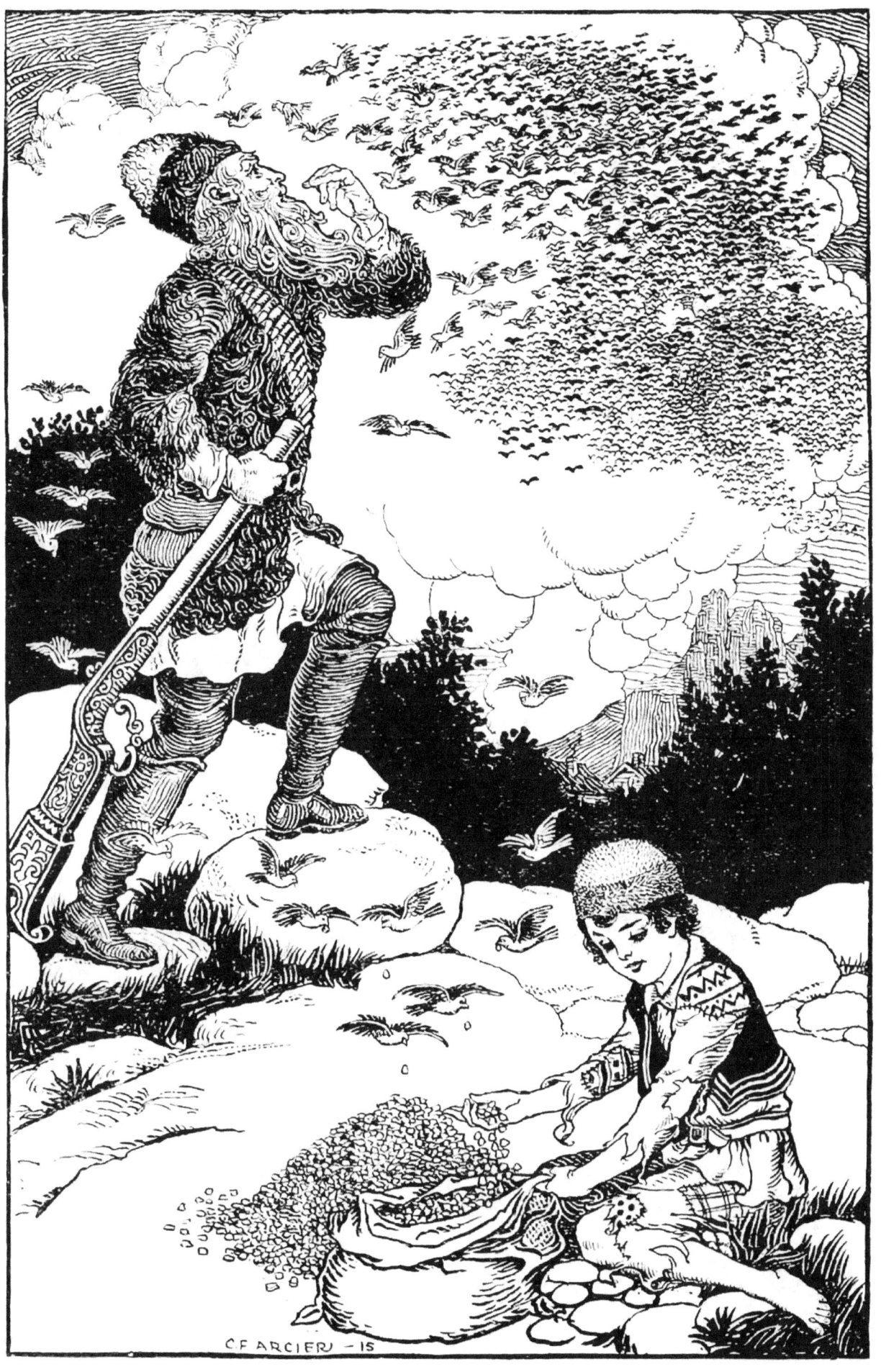

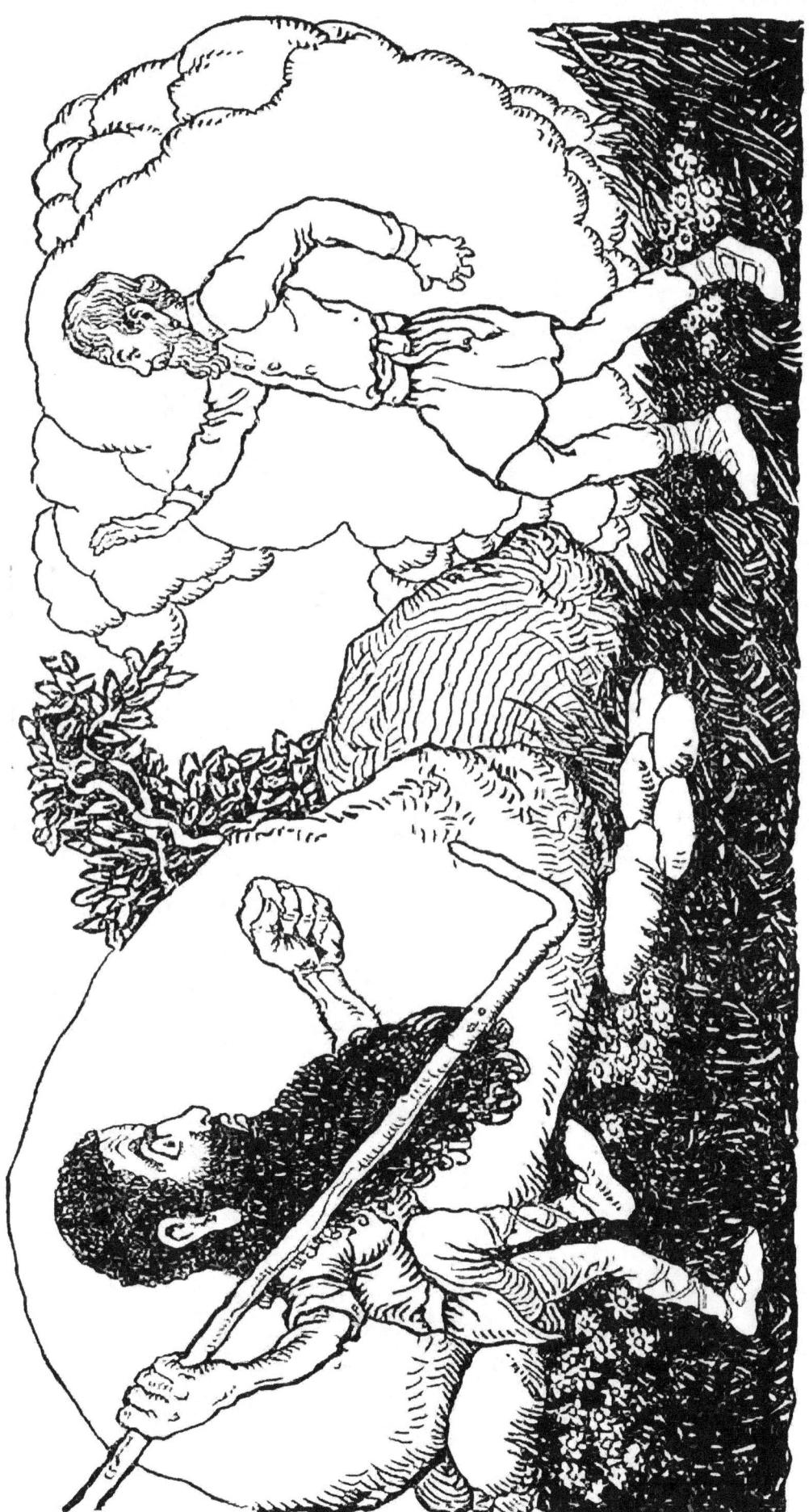

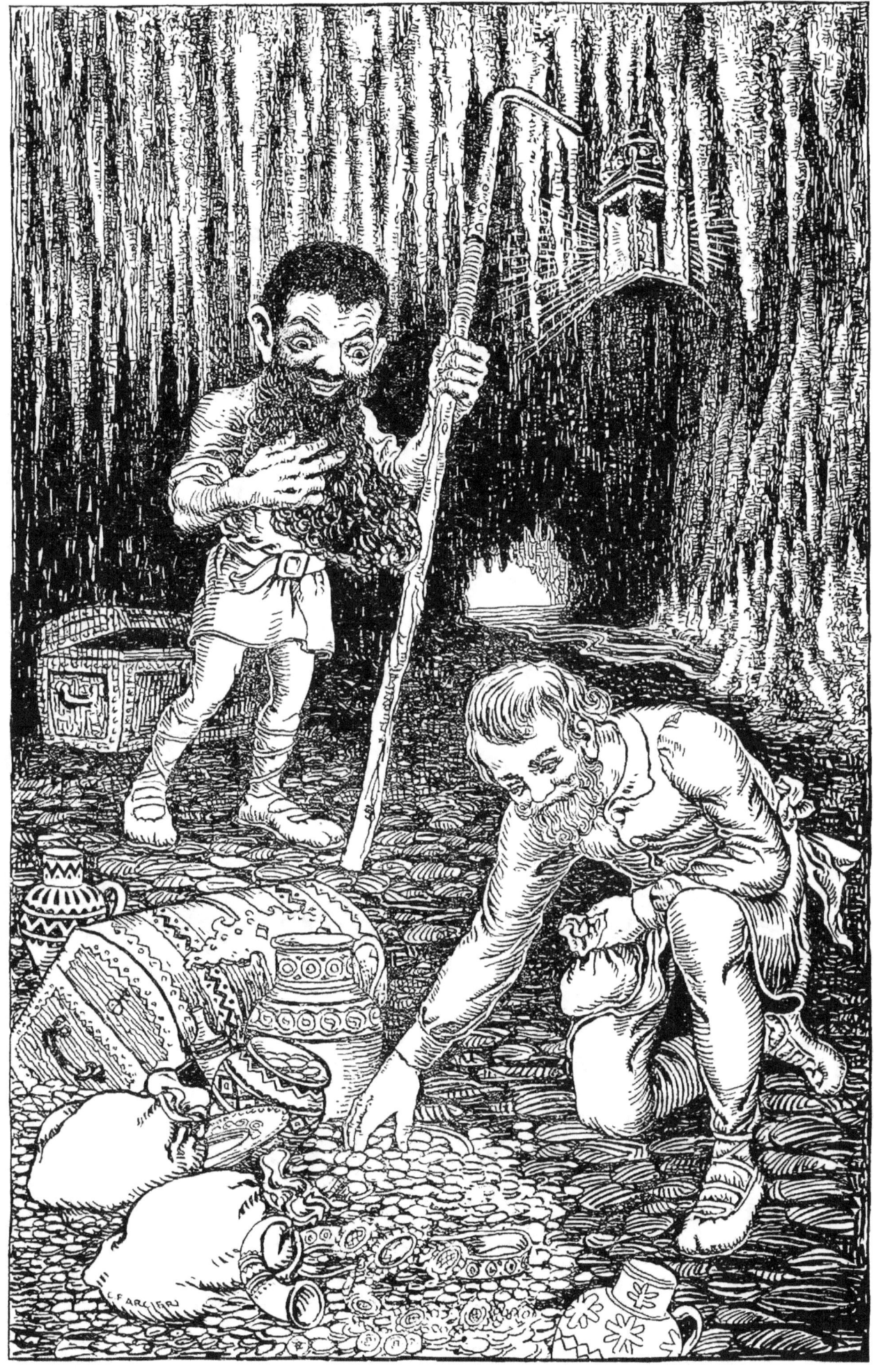

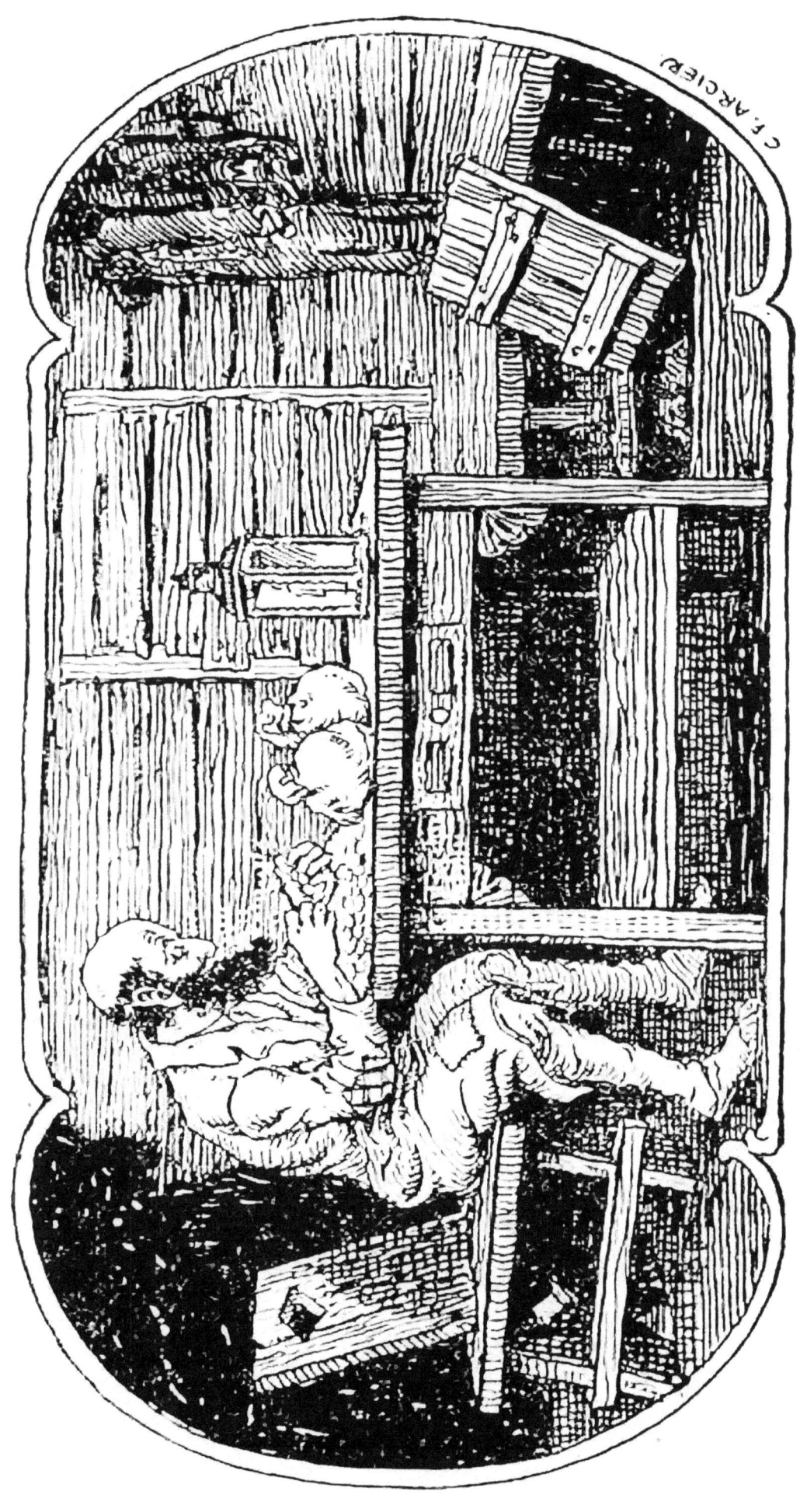

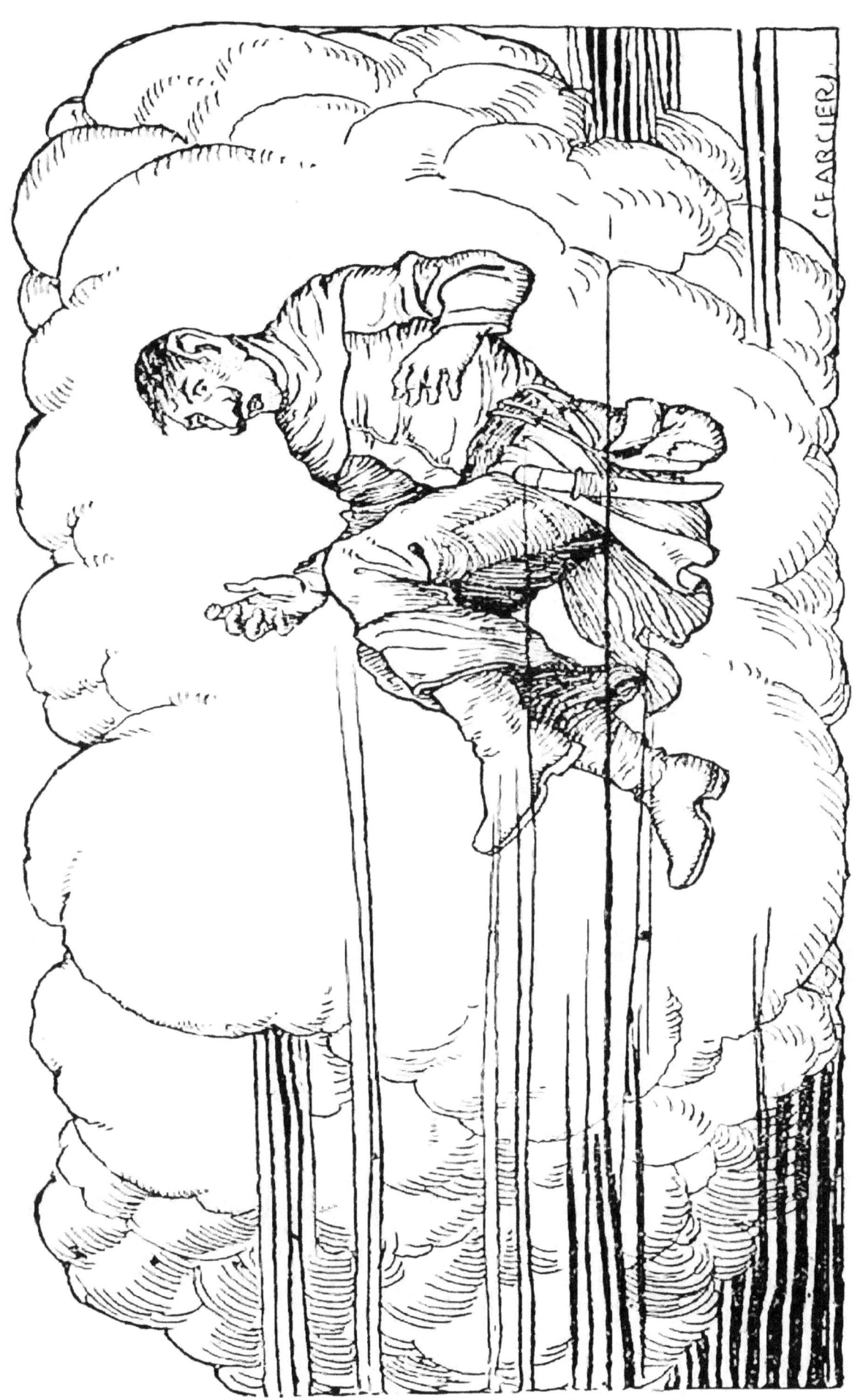

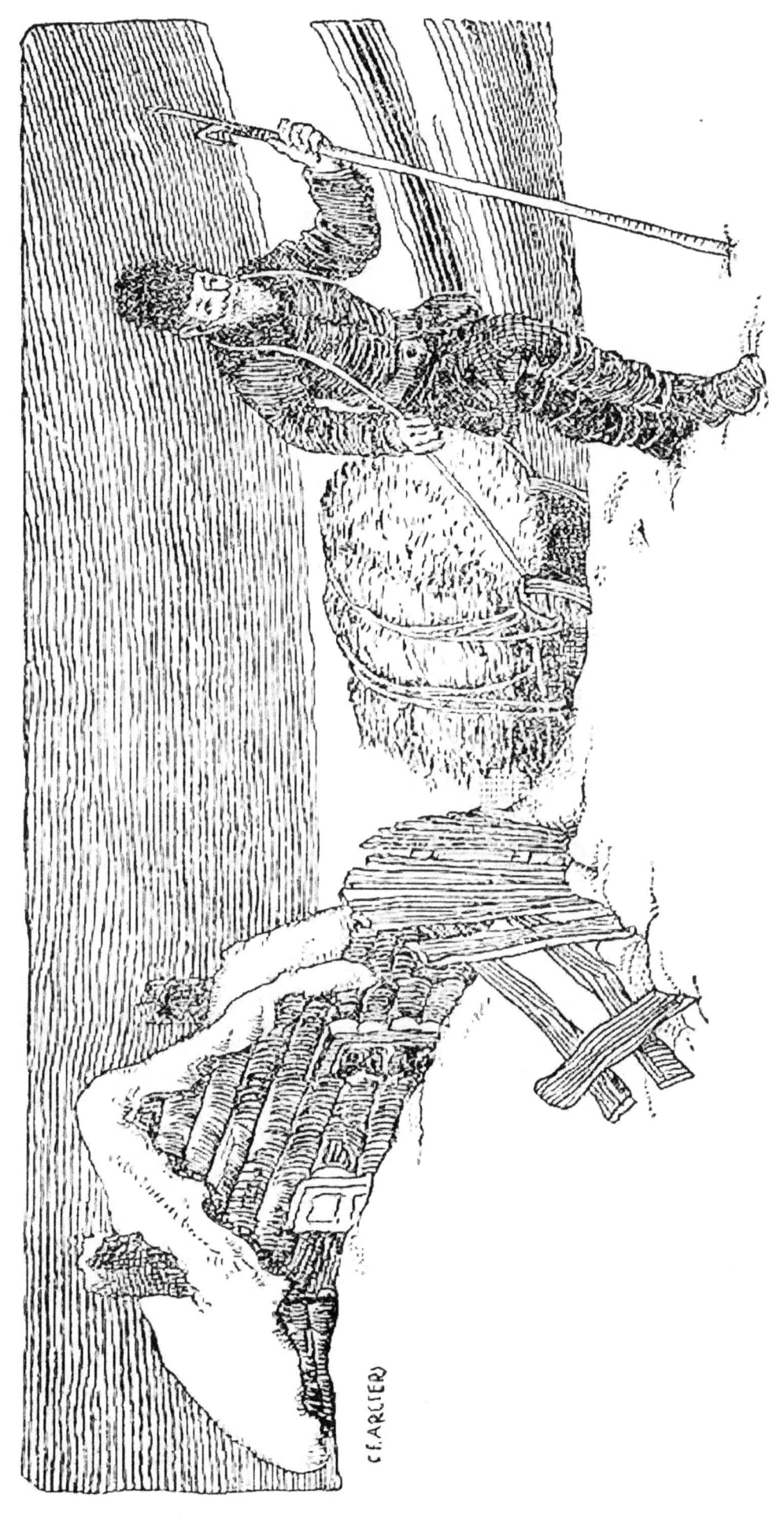

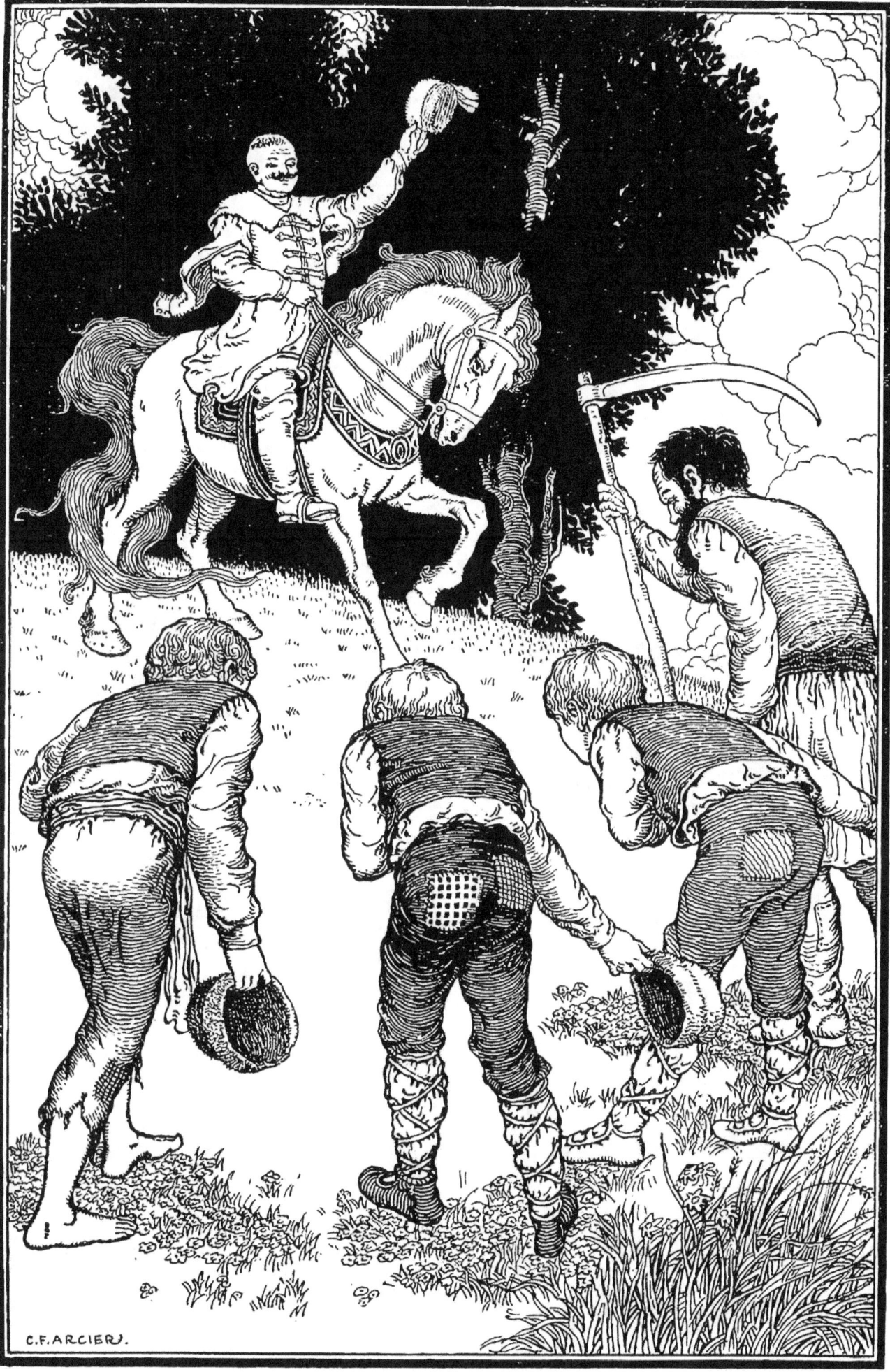

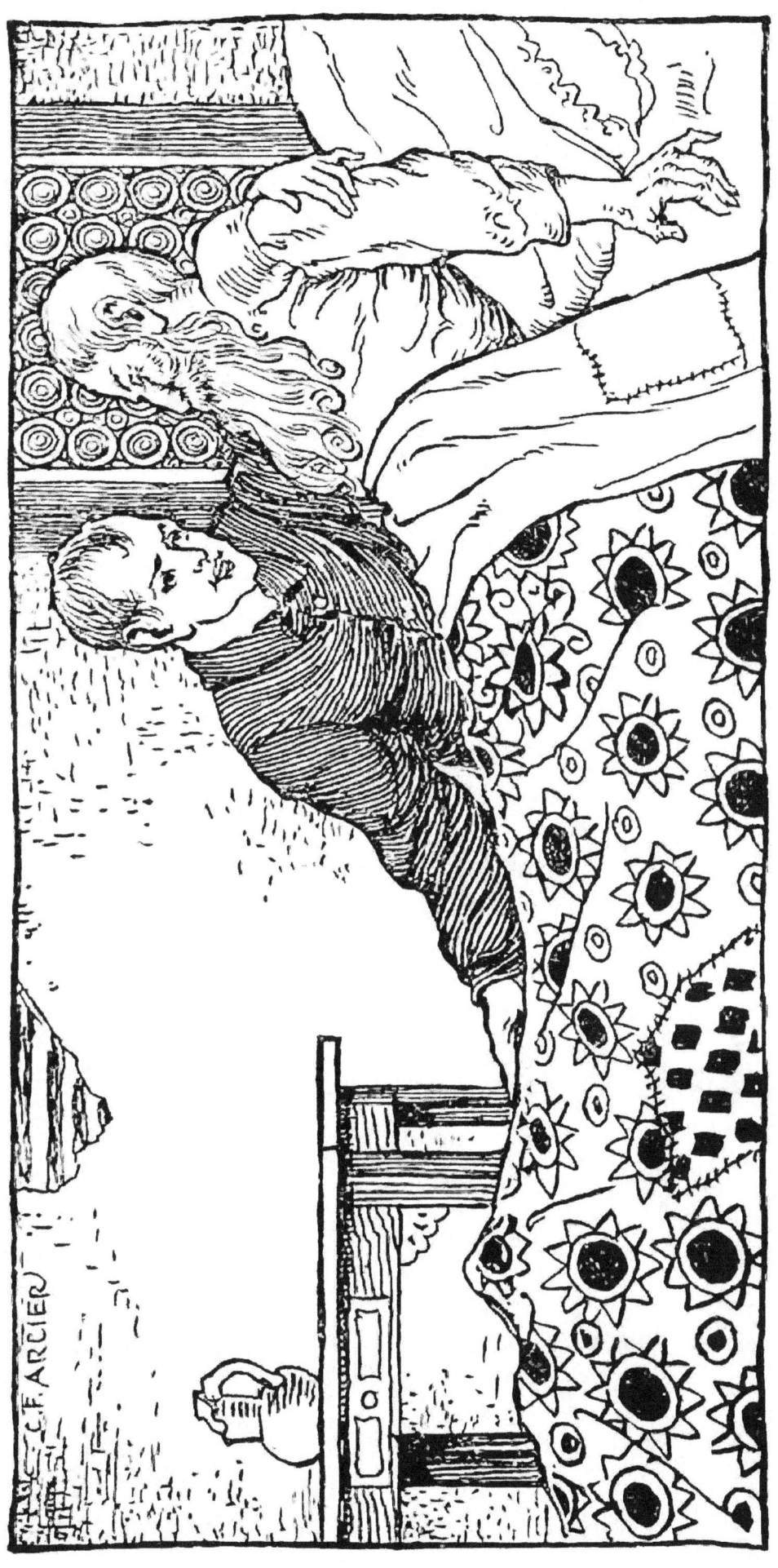

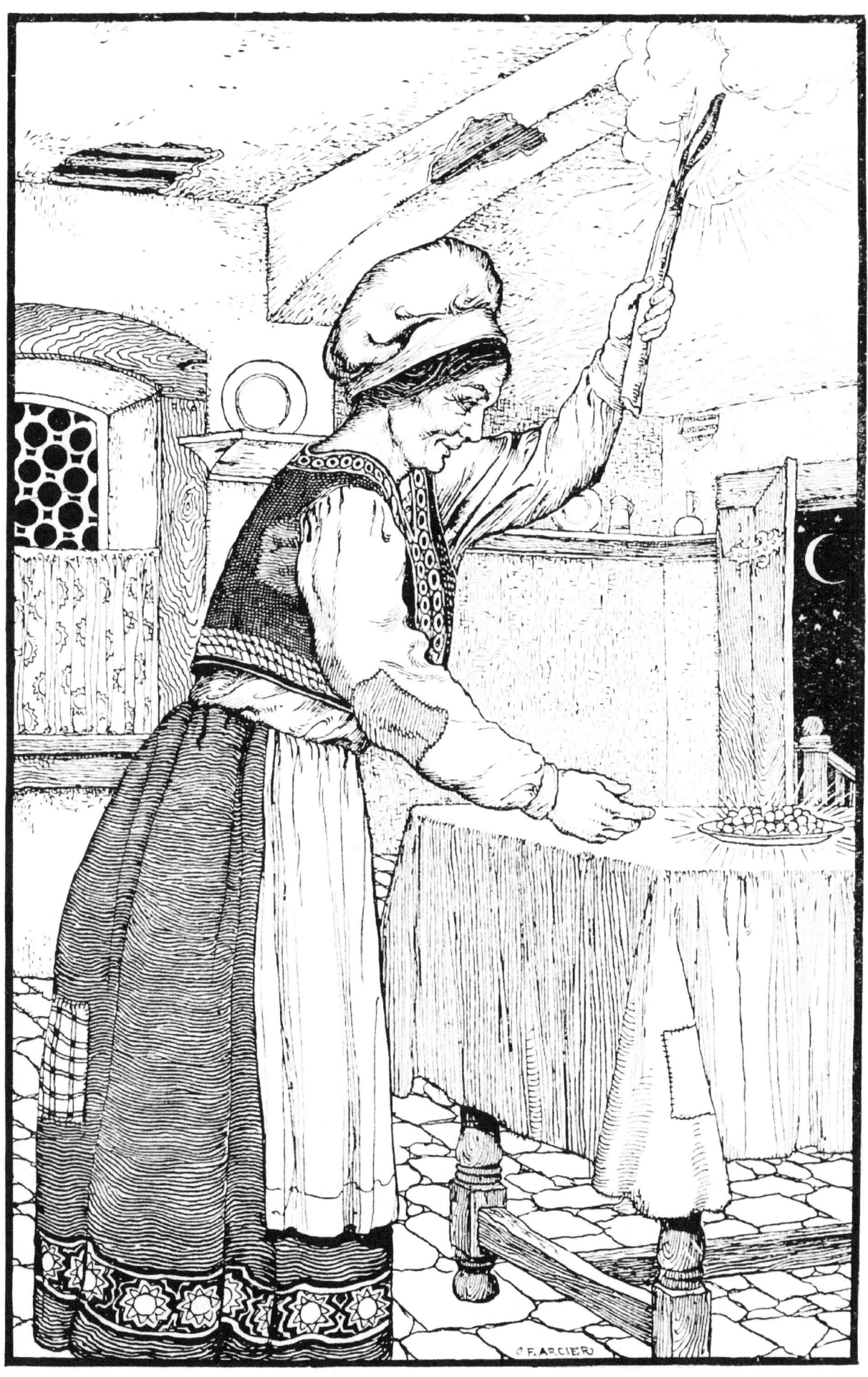

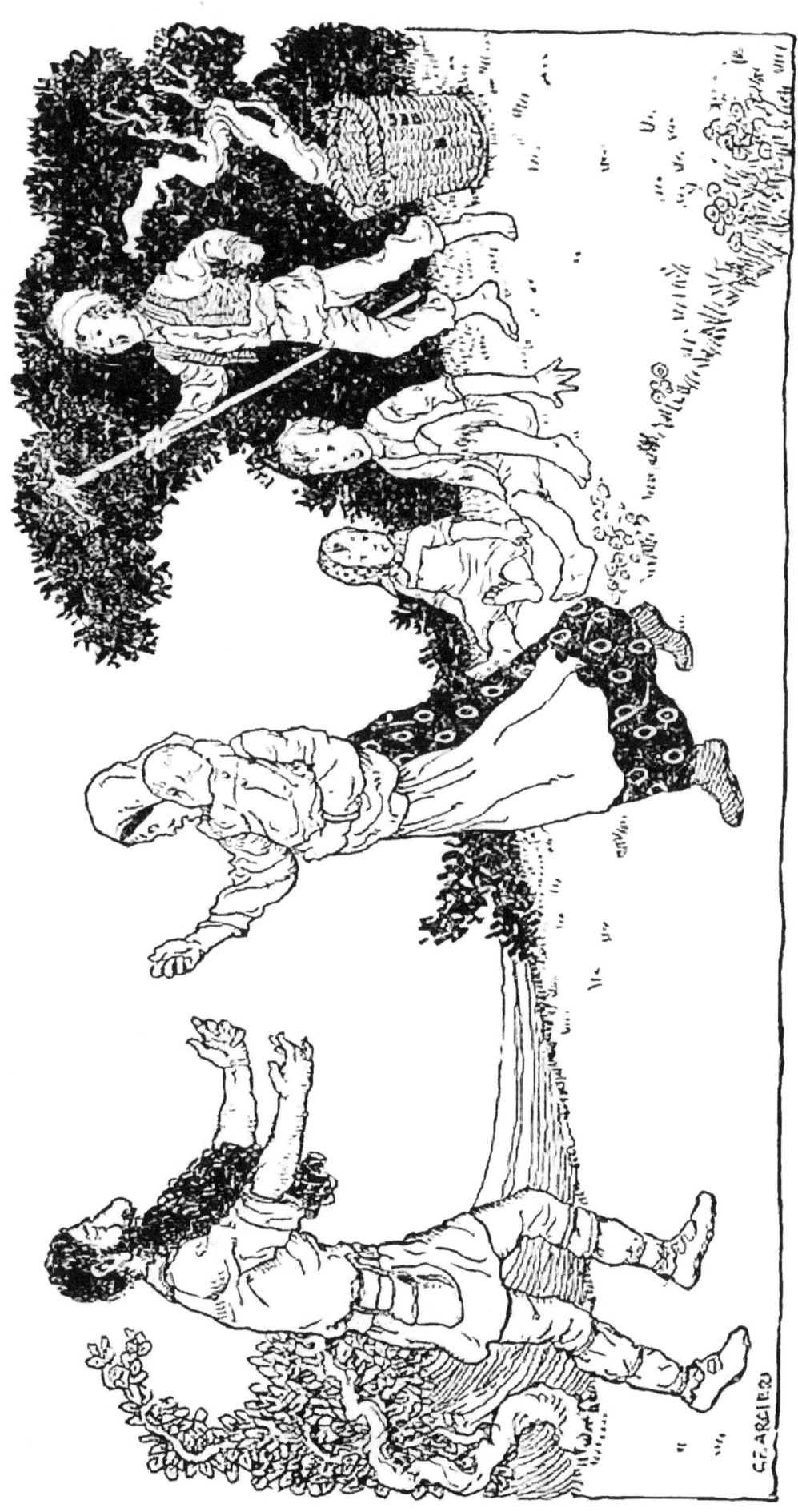

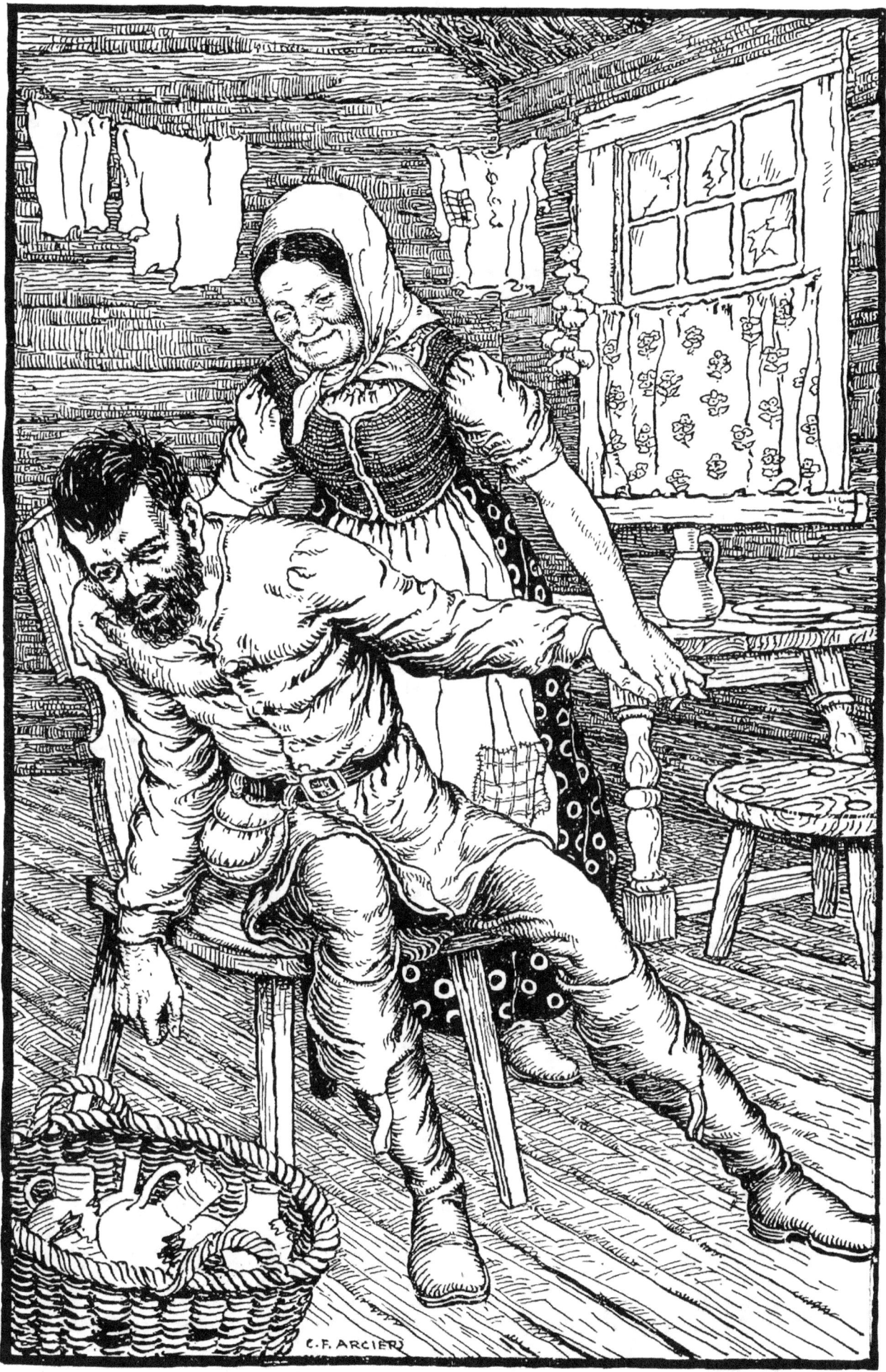

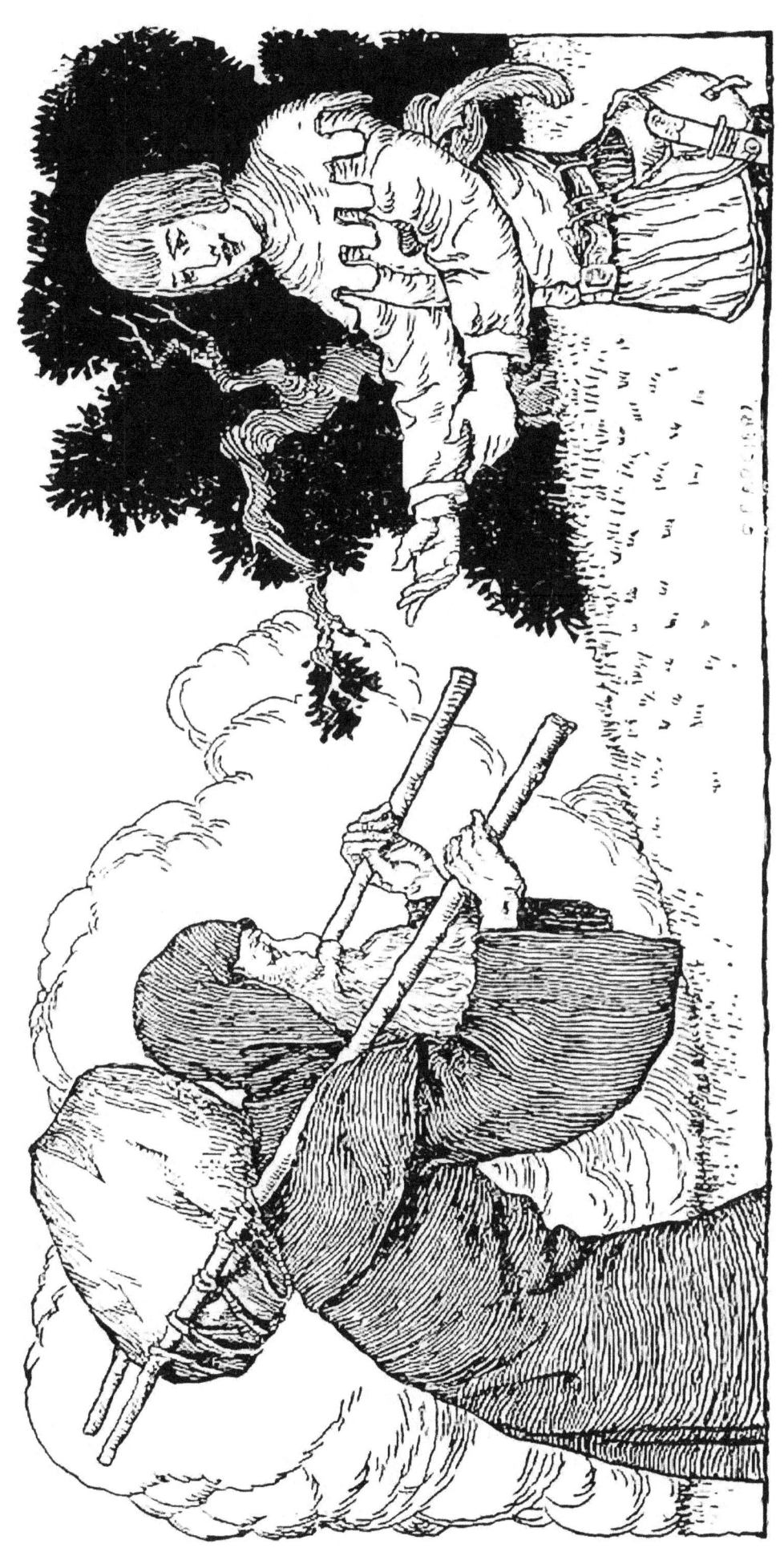

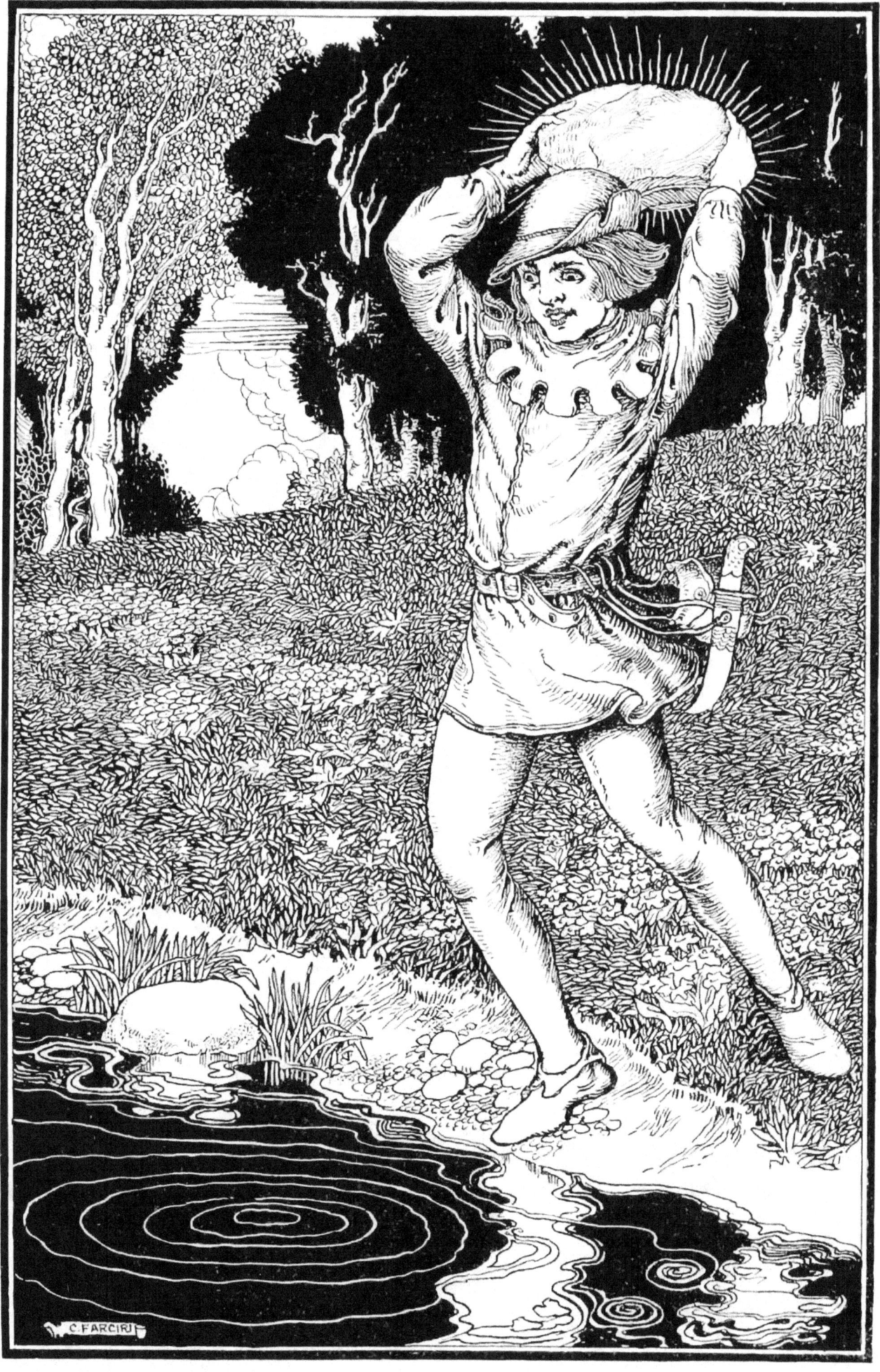

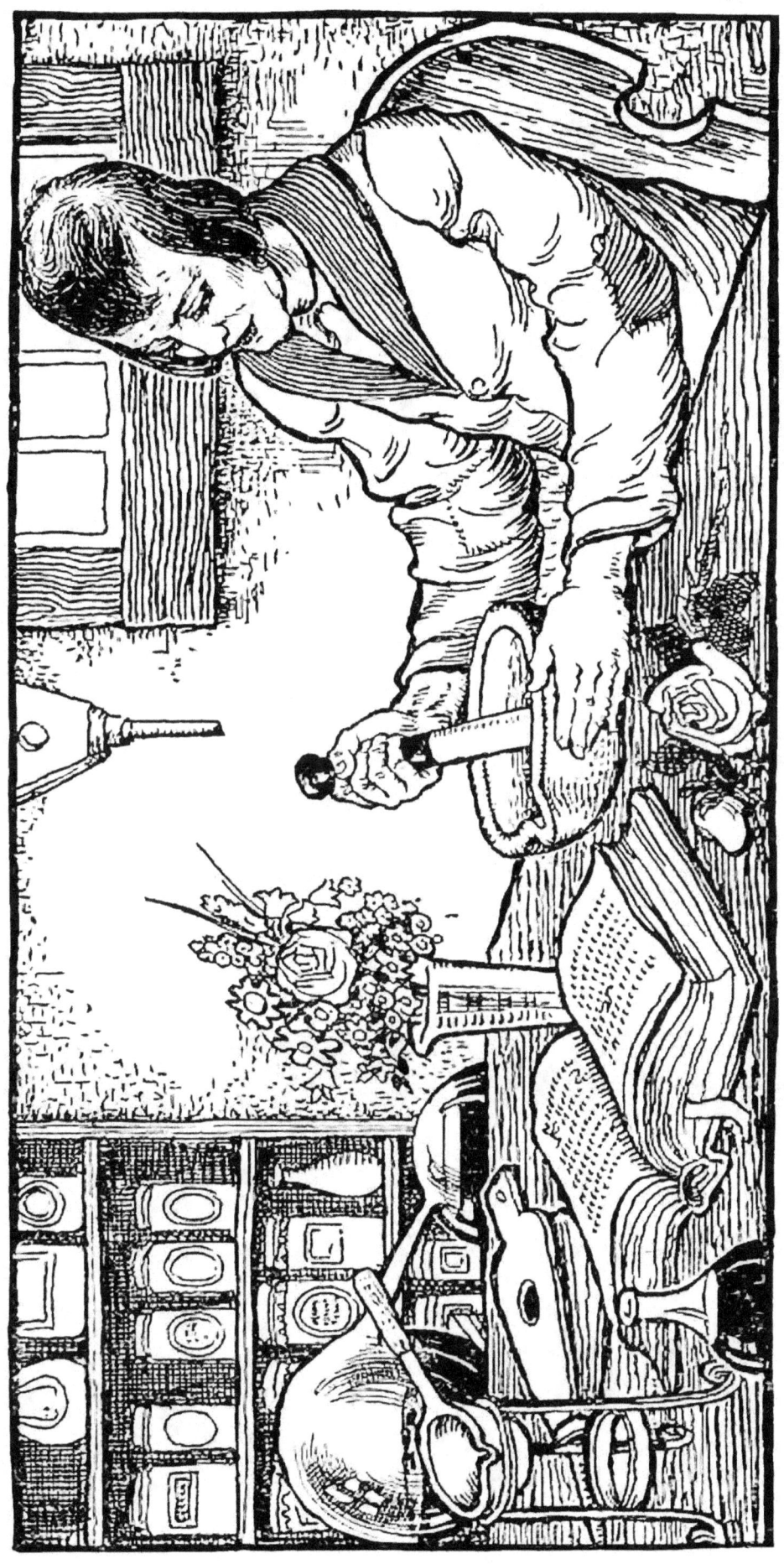

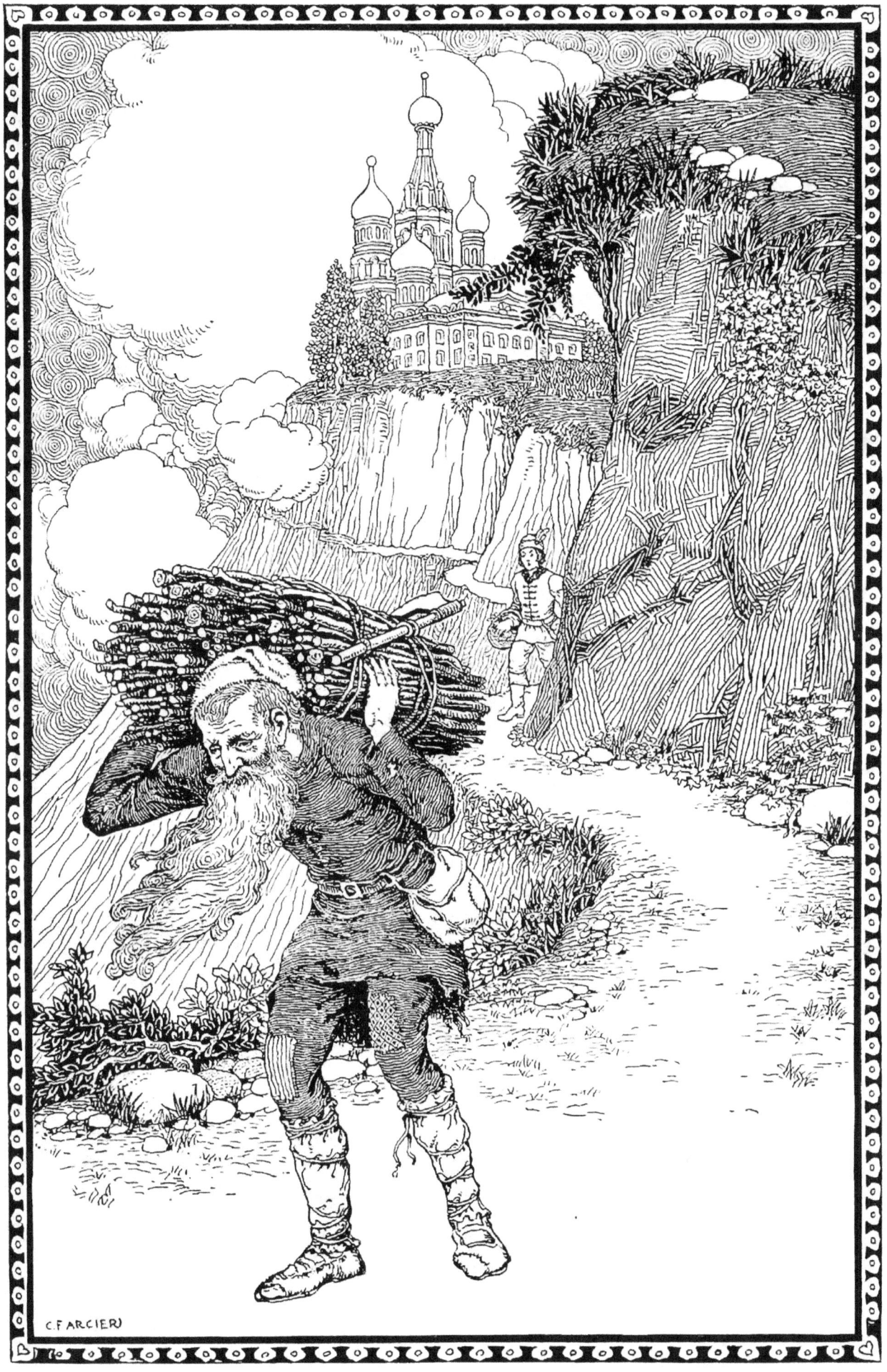

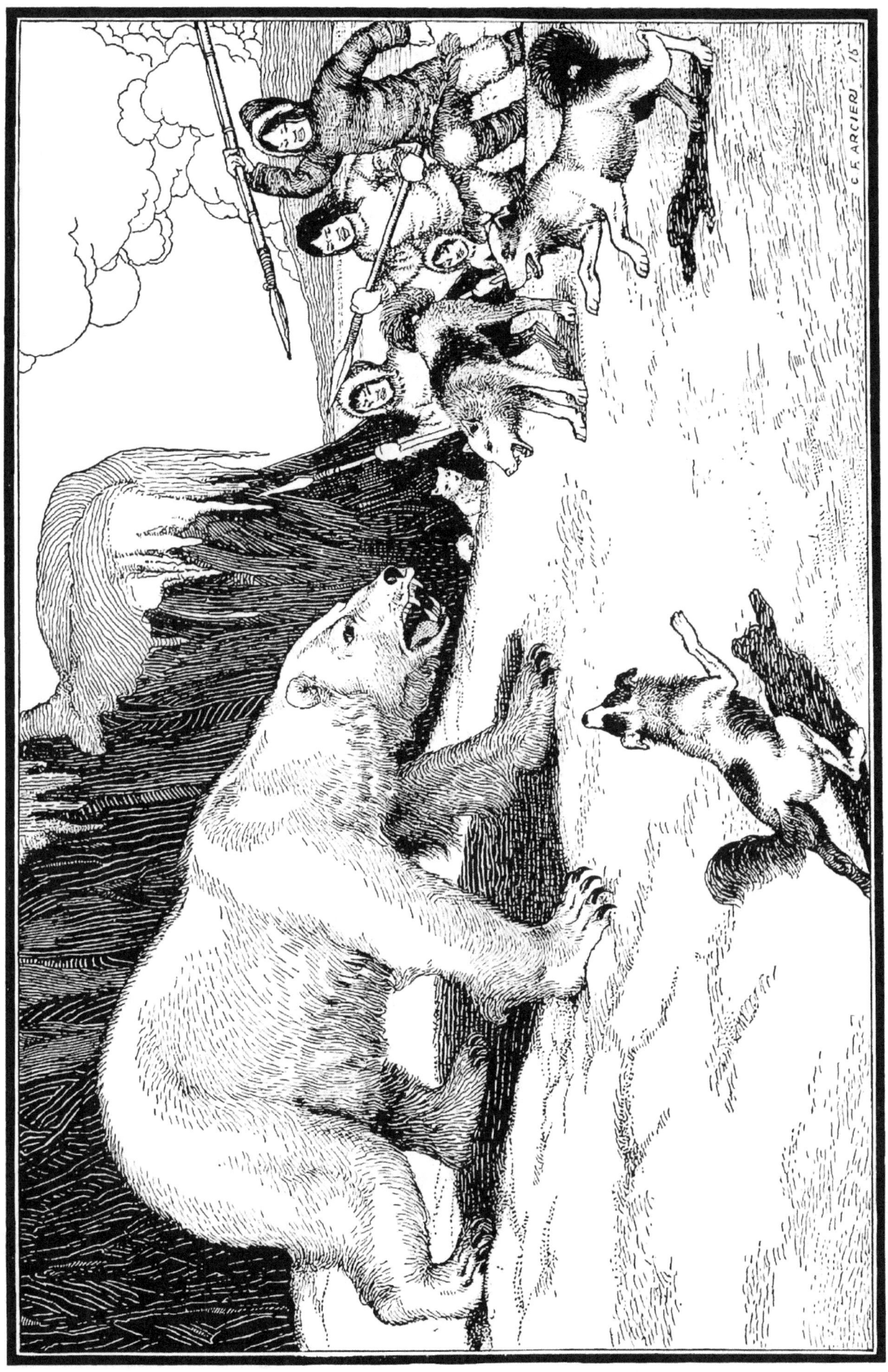

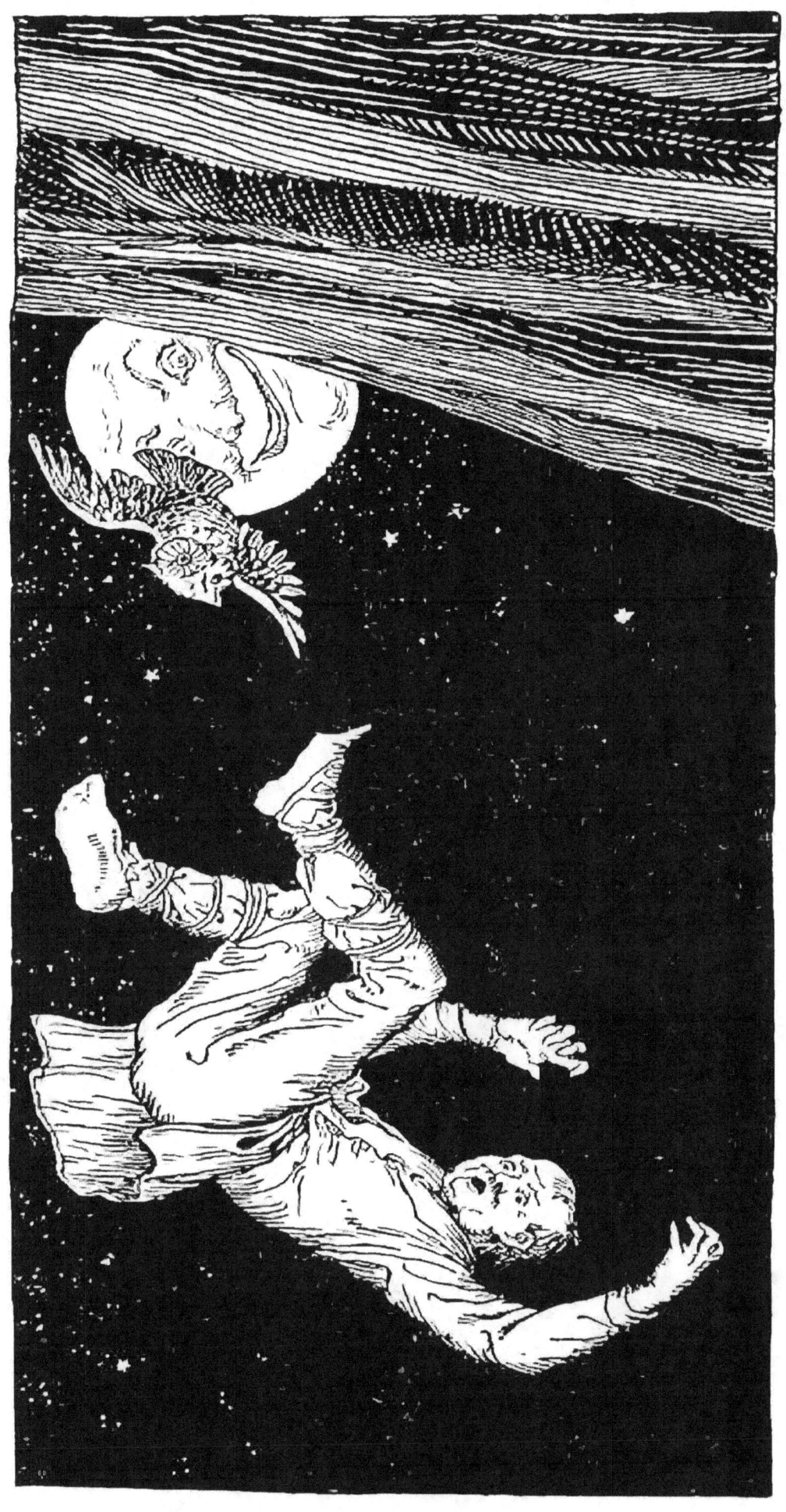

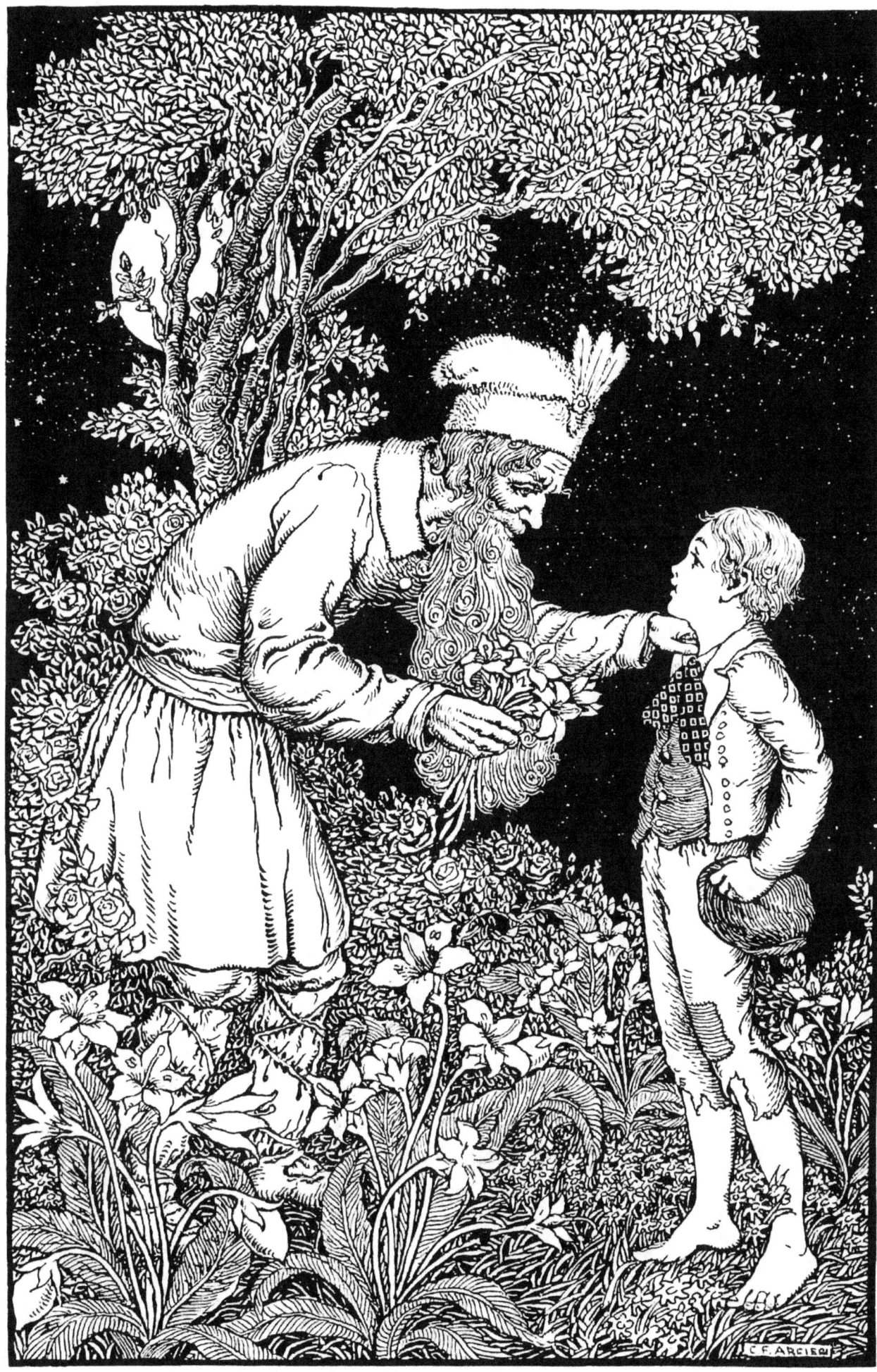

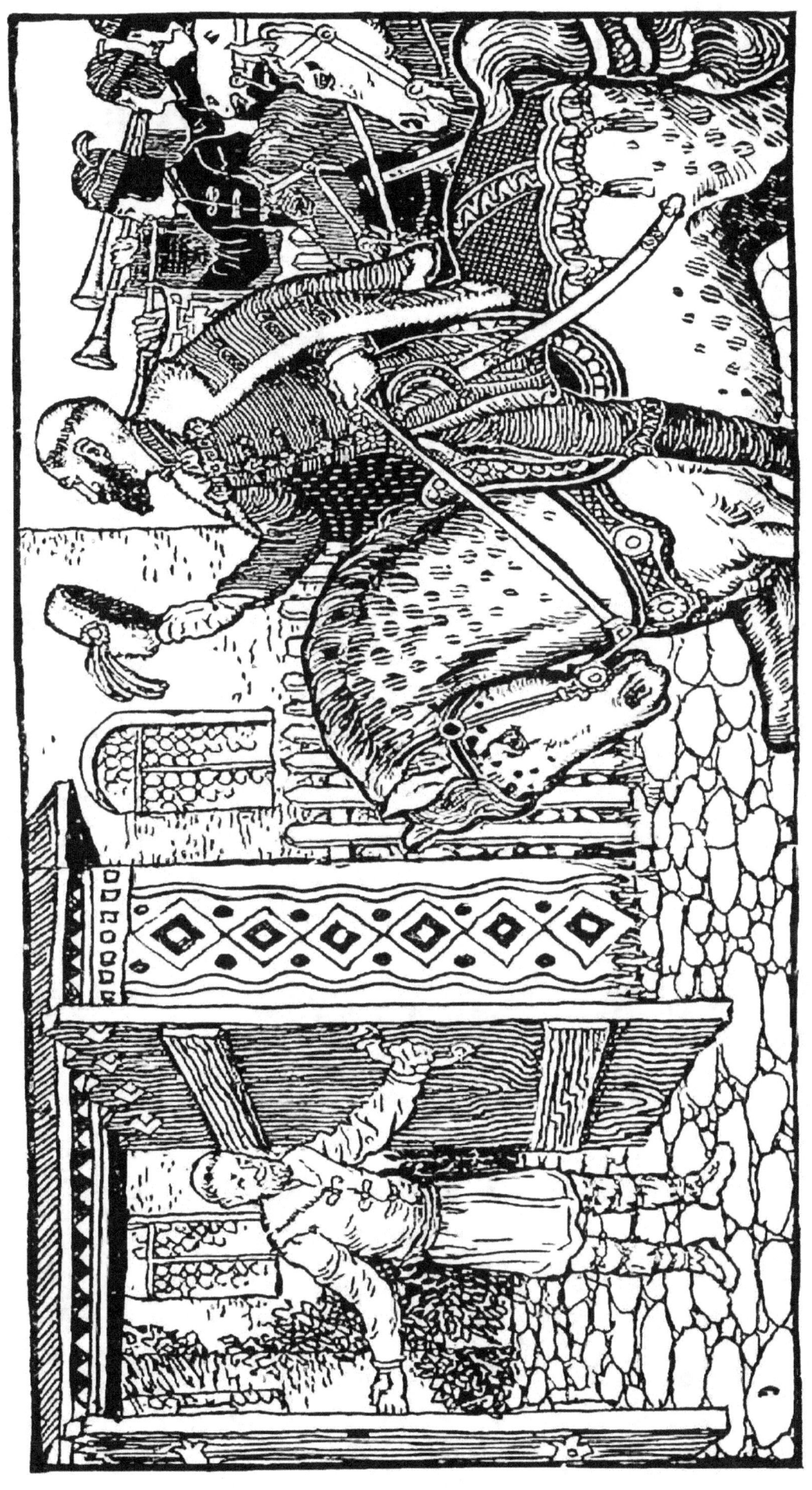

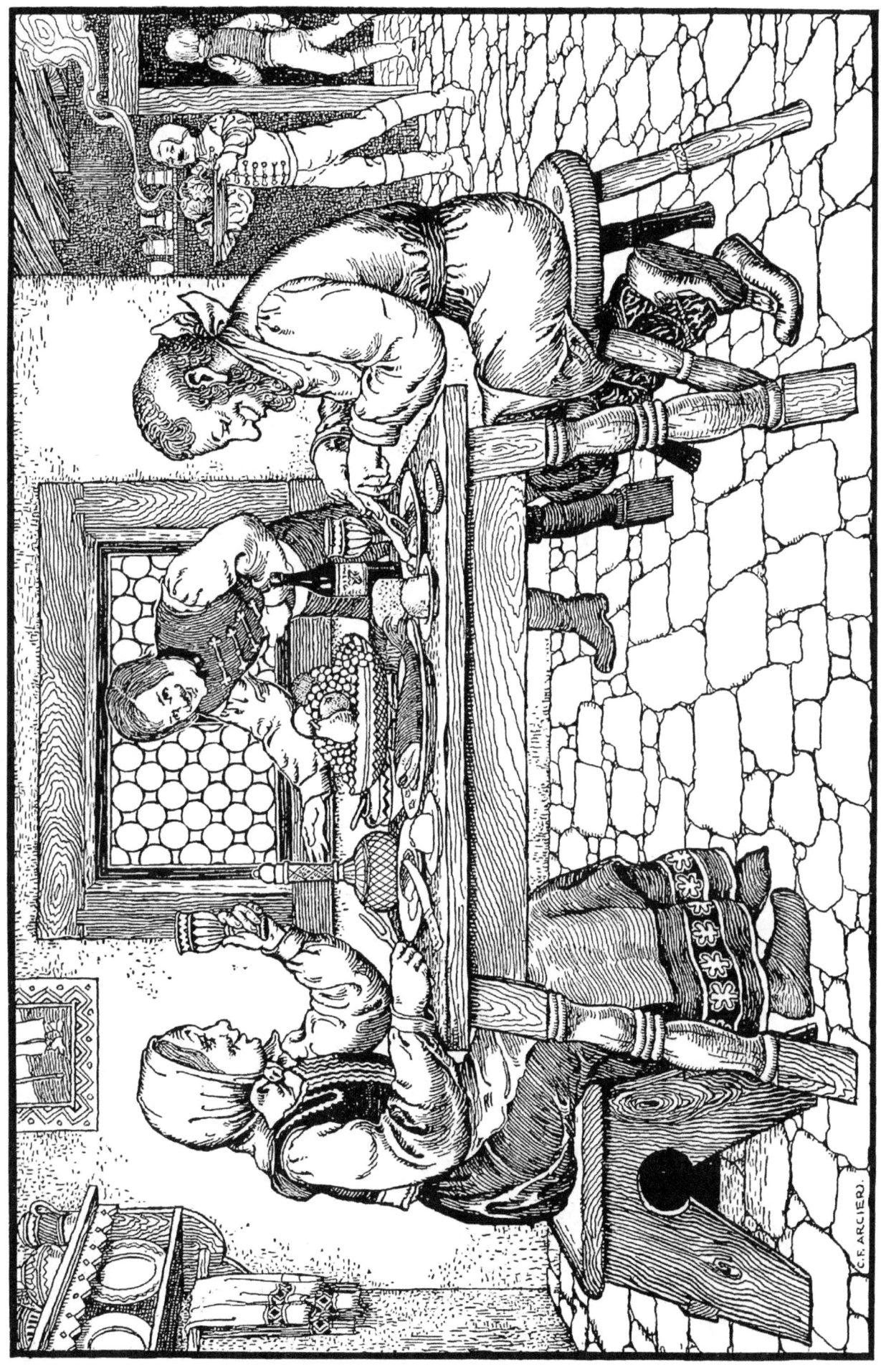

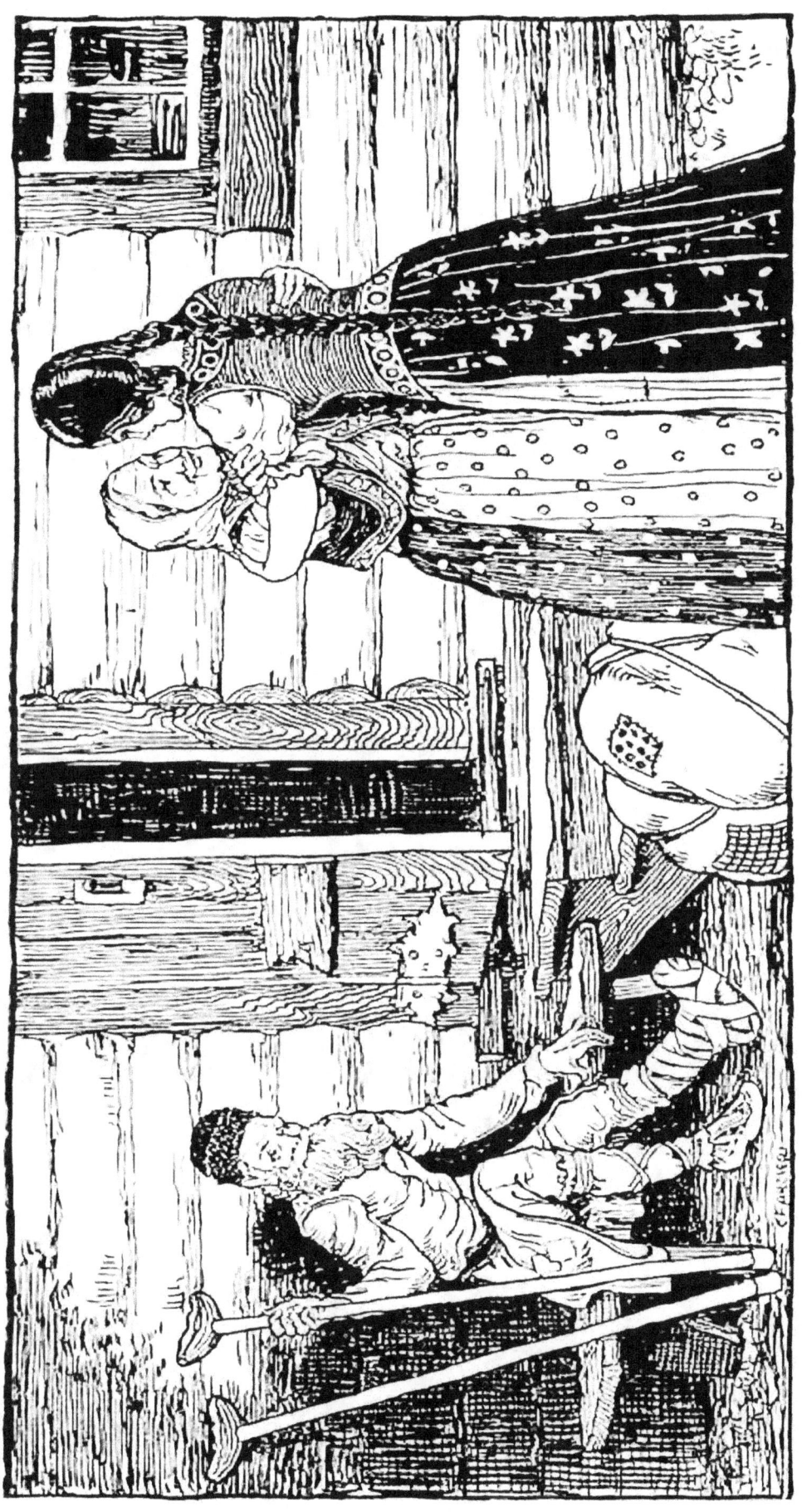

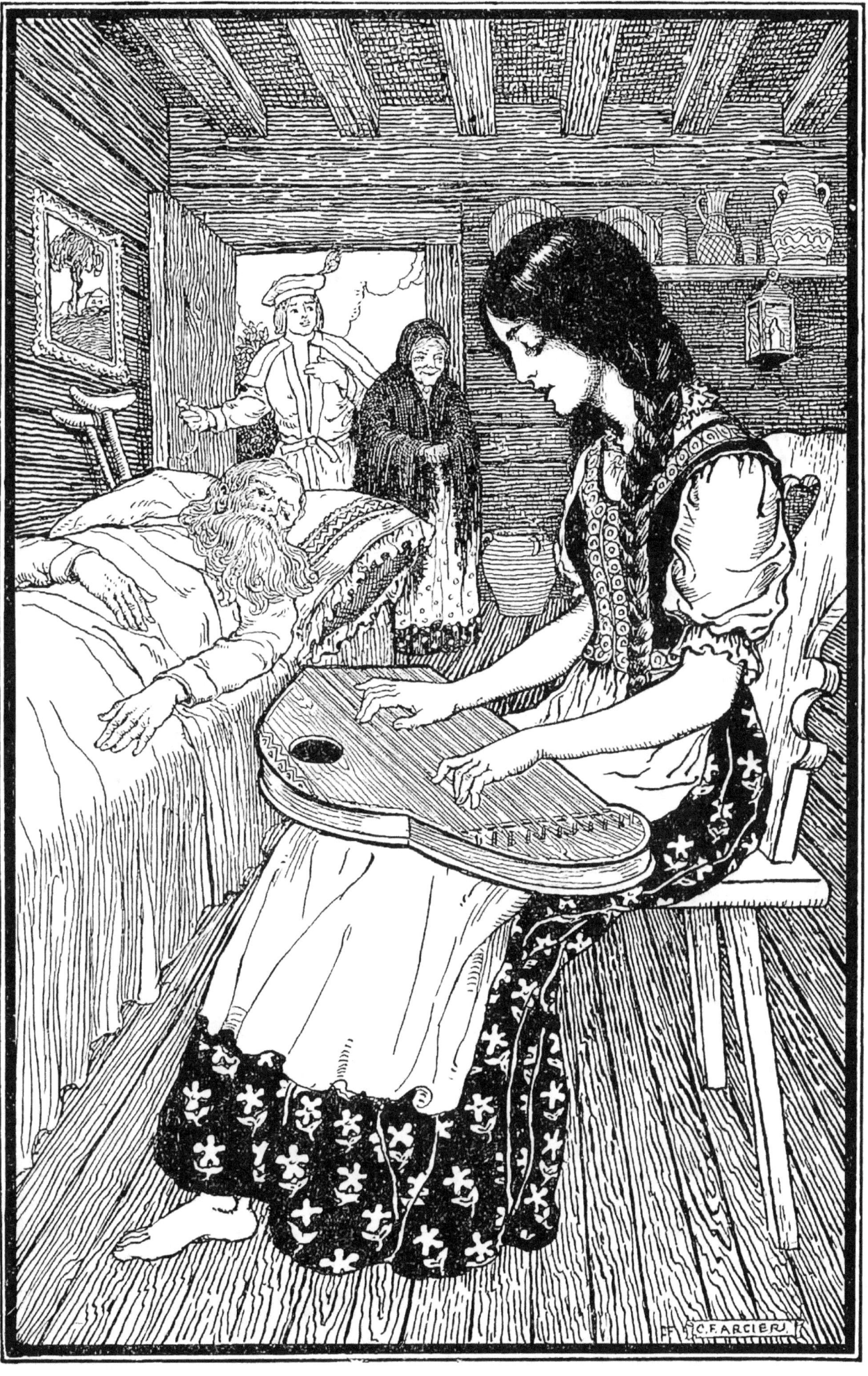

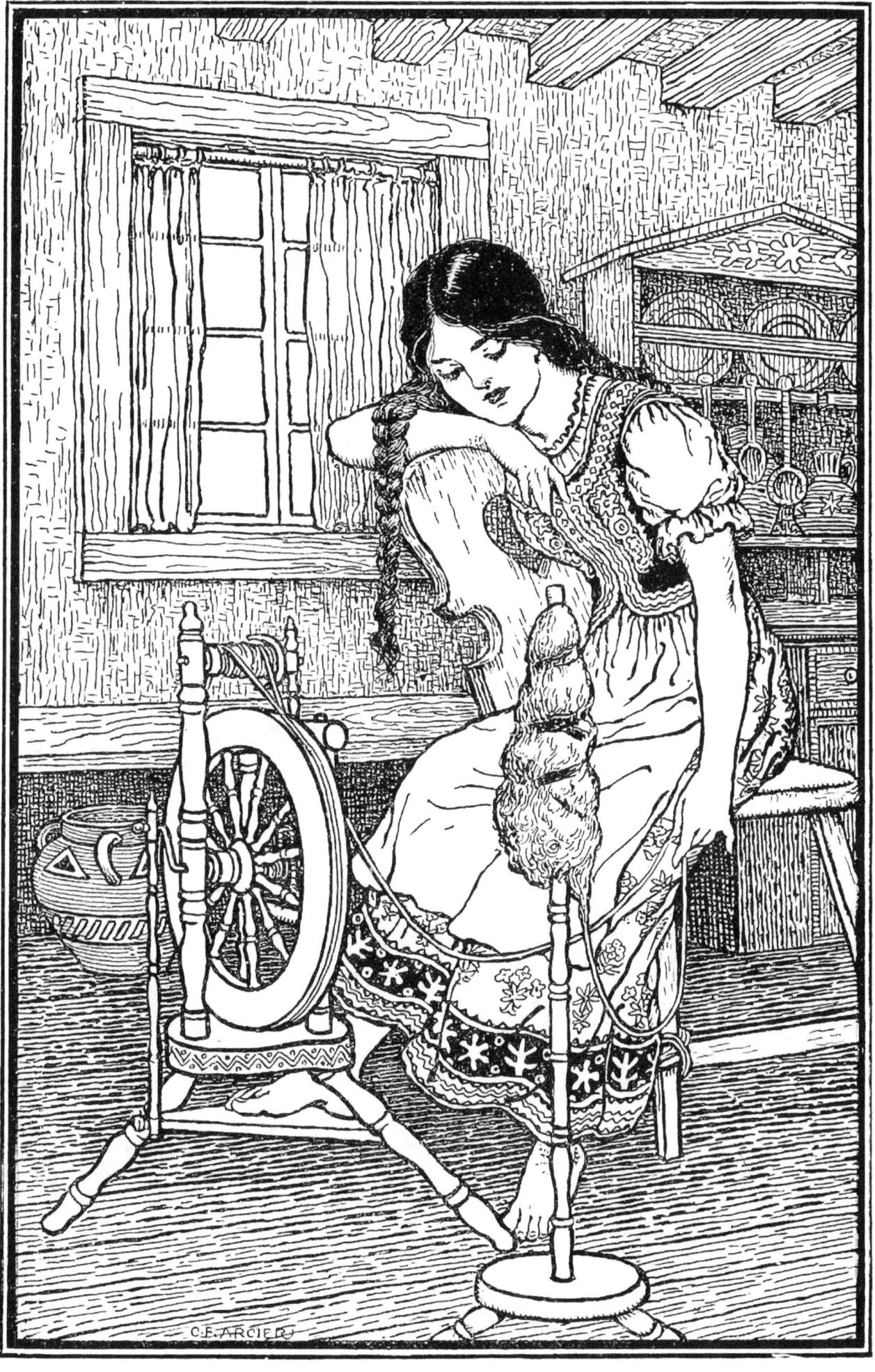

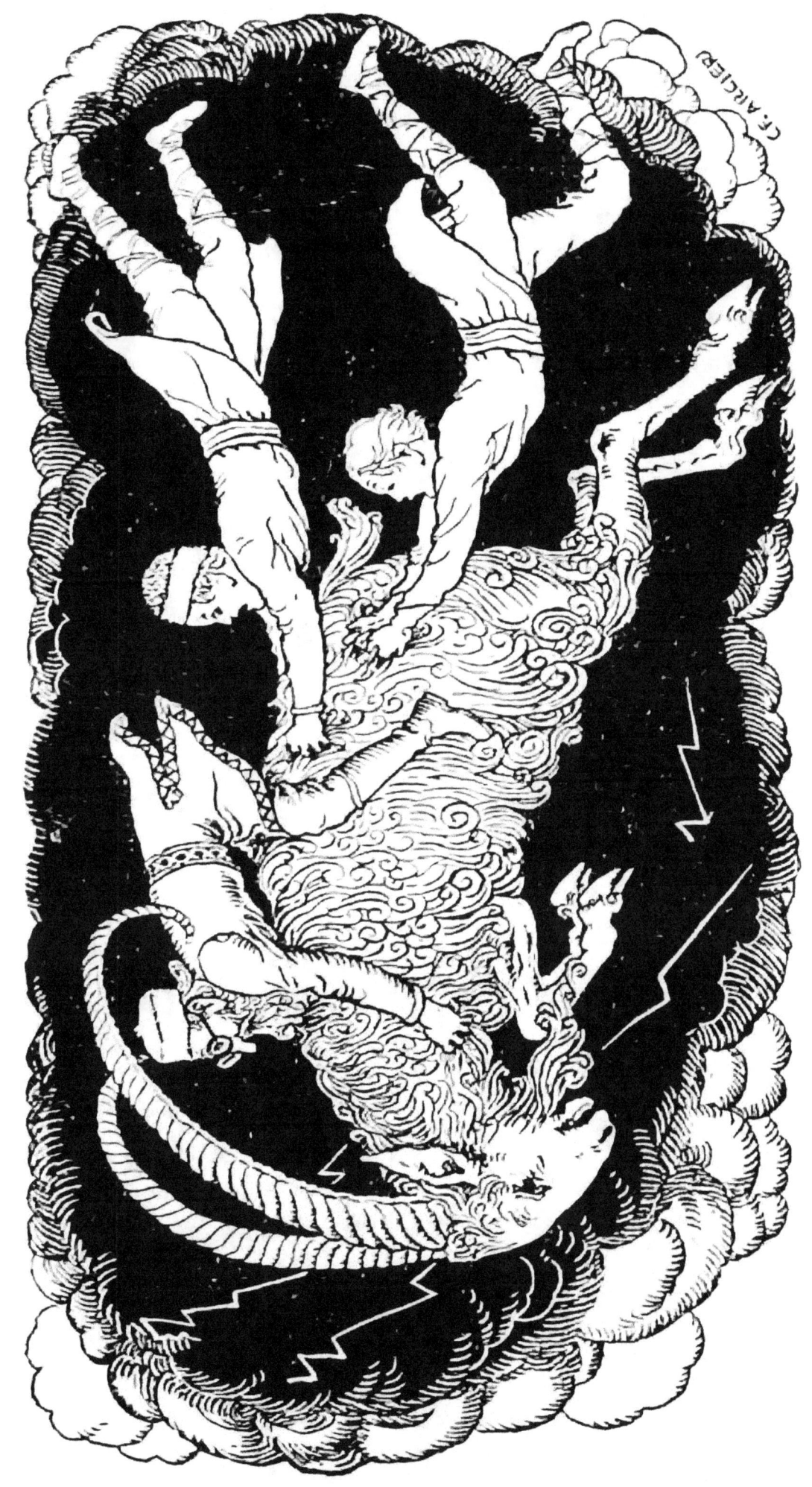

OTHER COLORING BOOKS YOU MAY LIKE:

Coloring Book of Vintage Caricatures and Characters

Coloring Book of Paisley and Patterns: An Intricate Coloring Book

Flowers: A Floral Inspiration Coloring Book

BadASS Buttocks: A Coloring Book for Adults

Fun, Fantasy and Fairy Tales: A Kid's Coloring Book

www.ingramcontent.com/pod-product-compliance
Lightning Source LLC
Chambersburg PA
CBHW081851170526

45167CB00007B/2965